Green-Light Your Book

Green-Light Your Book

HOW WRITERS CAN SUCCEED
IN THE NEW ERA OF PUBLISHING

Brooke Warner

Co-Founder/Publisher of She Writes Press

SHE WRITES PRESS

Published 2016
Printed in the United States of America
ISBN: 978-1-63152-802-6
E-ISBN: 978-1-63152-803-3
Library of Congress Control Number: 2016930397

Cover design by Julie Metz Ltd./metzdesign.com
Interior design by Tabitha Lahr

For information, address:
She Writes Press
1569 Solano Ave #546
Berkeley, CA 94707

She Writes Press is a division of SparkPoint Studio, LLC.

"Five Shades of Book Discovery," by Andrew Rhomberg, was originally published at DigitalBookWorld.com and is reprinted by permission of DBW and the author.

To my fellow She Writes Press authors,
trailblazers all of you.

Contents

Introduction

In late 2010, I was coming up on my ten-year anniversary in the publishing industry. I'd worked for two houses, one a small, family-run press with a couple of best sellers under its belt, the other an indie darling struggling to maintain its identity in the wake of having been gobbled up two separate times in less than ten years by bigger, corporate publishing houses. I loved my job working for the indie darling, but it was also depressing to witness how our corporate parent was diluting the press's very "indie-ness" in its push to make it more mainstream. It was a slow morph, but deliberate, and my mandate from up top was clear: be more commercial.

If you don't know what it means to "be more commercial," then bless you. But by the time you're finished with this book, you will know, and you will understand why what's most important in determining whether you get a book deal from a traditional house has nothing to do with how good your book actually is and everything to do with how commercial your book (and by extension you, your idea, your vision, your brand) is or has the potential to be.

I remember the book I had to reject that was the final straw in my traditional publishing career. It's less important what the subject matter was and more that it was a book that needed to be published. It was cutting edge and important, and its message was different from anything else our imprint had published into that category. I was disappointed by the no that was handed down, and my boss could see it on my face. She paused and made me a thoughtful offer: I could acquire it. I'd been there long enough and had "money in the bank," so to speak, but if it didn't "work" (i.e., at least earn out its advance), the failure would be on me.

Considering the statistic that 97 percent of all books fail (meaning they don't earn out said advance), you can imagine where my mind went. Could this little book defy the odds and be the 3 percent? What kind of money would I have to offer to ensure that the book earned out? And if I made a lowball offer to cover my bases, what message would that send to the author, or to my own entire company, for that matter? I was stuck. A good offer put me in a vulnerable position, and a low offer put me in a somewhat more vulnerable position. So I chickened out. Or maybe I realized the clock was ticking for me and that I wasn't going to last in traditional publishing much longer.

Later that week, I made a bid on another book I had far less passion for. It's not so important what the subject matter of that book was, either, but it was a book that did not need to be published. It offered nothing new. It would be going into a crowded shelving category, but its message was packaged and tied with a pretty little bow. The author had a celebrity connection and a big-shot agent. I was not elated when I got the go-ahead to make the offer. Though it was the biggest offer I had ever made in my publishing career, I was deflated by the fact that this honor was going to this particular book, and that for this reason it would be forever set apart from anything else I'd acquired during my ten-plus years in book publishing.

These two experiences ushered in the end of my traditional publishing career. My faith in traditional publishing as the shaper and keeper of all our culture holds dear had been eroding for some time. I sometimes wondered what an acquiring editor who'd come of age at Random House or Simon & Schuster in the 1930s and '40s would have thought of all the reality-TV tie-in books being put out now by these two houses, which once published literary icons like William Faulkner, James Joyce, and Laura Z. Hobson. And this isn't about snobbery; for me, it's about how far publishers have moved away from publishing what matters and toward publishing what sells.

Despite that big revelation, I can't say I blame them. Publishing houses are businesses. Are we allowed to begrudge them their effort to make a profit? Maybe, but let's not. Let's cut them some slack. However, if we know that their models are about money, and data-driven to the extent to which they can be, and all about assessing author platform (which I'll write about extensively in Chapter 3), and placing much more emphasis on the author's media connections than on the content of the book itself, should we continue to look to big publishing as the be-all and end-all? I think not. Readers have stopped looking to the big houses to be the curators of the lists they want to read, and yet aspiring authors have not made this shift and instead still yearn for the validation of being on a big press, though it's a privilege that comes with some strings attached (which we'll explore in Chapter 1).

But back to my story of leaving traditional publishing, which finally happened in 2012, just as that book I'd made such a big offer on was going into production. I waited more than a full year after passing on the book I really wanted to acquire as I tried to figure out what my next steps were going to be. By late 2011, it was clear that I would stay in publishing, but I wanted to leave for something I could stand behind. I wanted to start a publishing company that allowed me to say yes to those books I was having to reject, books that rested on their laurels but didn't necessarily come with celebrity endorsements. The company I envisioned would publish books based on their merit alone, and it wouldn't matter whether they were commercial or whether the author had a platform. And so, in 2012, I cofounded She Writes Press with Kamy Wicoff, founder of SheWrites.com. It was shaped and formed within the parameters that drew me to publishing in the first place, as well as a little bit in response to traditional publishing. And while I don't in any way have it out for traditional publishing, it wouldn't be honest to say I'm not disappointed by what it's become.

Kamy and I started what we call a hybrid publishing company, where the authors invest in their own work up front for a higher percentage of the profits on the tail end. And while we are what the industry calls "author-subsidized," She Writes Press is not a self-publishing company, and the authors who publish with us are not self-published authors. In the years since She Writes Press launched, I've gone head-to-head with some of the biggest players in the traditional space in an effort to explain what we are doing—and also why it's necessary. And we are not alone. There are many other nontraditional models like ours, and countless "indie" authors who've co-opted a label that once belonged to small, "independent" (but traditional) publishing houses. And I say more power to them, because the indie-author movement has gained so much traction that self-publishing (or paying to publish in general) has gone from being stigmatized to earning legitimacy through proven gains.

Yet we have not fully arrived. The playing field is not level yet. The rise of self-publishing has led the industry to realize two things about self-published authors: 1) it's not going to get rid of them; and 2) there's money to be made off them. Because there exist two separate camps—the traditionally published authors and everyone else—those of us who fall into the "everyone else" category will be taken advantage of and undervalued unless we advocate for ourselves and also learn how to subvert the system while working within it (which is the focus of Chapter 7).

When I left traditional publishing in 2012, I was leaving an industry that I believed had lost its imperative. It may have been moralistic on my part, but I was also grieving what I felt I'd lost—which was being able to acquire books that contributed something important to the cultural conversation. To be sure, traditional publishing is still putting out books that do that, but I also know there are editors sitting in their offices, just like I was back then, being told to go out and get "big books," which means commercial, which means celebrity driven or sound bite–y or hyperpackaged or dumbed down. Because those are the books that sell.

If you're reading this book, you may still be holding on to the dream of being traditionally published, and that's fine. I'm not here to change your mind; rather, I'm here to open your eyes to the bigger picture of publishing outside the small square that traditional publishing occupies. Maybe you already have your doubts about getting picked up by an agent or a publishing house, and you secretly know your book is really, really awesome, and you're peeved that those chances feel so slim. This book is for you. Or maybe you've already written off traditional publishing, but you're scared about what it's going to cost you to get published and you're not sure what to do or how to approach it. You are overwhelmed by the choices, but you want to publish well, and you want to understand what you're getting into and the potential return on your investment. Yes, this book is for you, too.

Above and beyond all else, this book is about saying yes. It's about moving past the desire or the need to have someone else validate you as worthy. I'm going to show you to whom you are turning over your power when you allow the publishing industry to mandate whether you "should" be published, and I'm going to dispel a few myths about traditional publishing's being the equivalent of hitting the literary jackpot. I'm also going to get into the nitty-gritty of what you need to know to be a successful author in today's publishing climate. This is about understanding sales and data and distribution (and I promise to deliver all of this in a super-palatable way), and it's also about being an author ambassador, which means paving the road for others to follow in your footsteps and making sure that your successes and failures alike help those who come after you to publish as well, or better.

You might be reading this book and feeling like you don't know if you're ready to green-light your own work yet, and that's okay. I never want to pressure any author into making a choice they are not ready to make. What I do hope to do, however, is help authors understand that in any other creative industry—

film, music, visual arts, fashion—green-lighting your own work is a sign of an independent spirit. In no other industry are you punished for giving your own work the stamp of approval. And while publishing is getting there, we are so not there yet. Which is why the more we say yes and the more we publish good work, the more we collectively turn up the dial. In doing so, we command the same treatment as our traditionally published counterparts.

As published authors, we have one fundamental thing in common: we are all published. To me, this is what matters most. The only thing holding any of us back from publishing, therefore, is the validation we may need to allow ourselves to take the next step. We may need a yes from an agent we admire, or a yes from the editor at the house we've always dreamed of publishing with. Others of us might be wise to listen to other kinds of yeses—the yes of a trusted editor, the yes of our beta readers, the yes of our partners if we're going to invest money we share. But the most important yes, regardless of how many other resounding yeses you might hear, or against the deafening lack of yeses you've wished for, is your own singular, solid, sure yes. You can do it. You can green-light your book. And be successful doing it.

Chapter 1.

The State of the Industry

In recent years, what happens in book publishing has often been national news. The players are celebrities in their own right—Amazon, Hachette, Penguin Random House. The news stories are gripping: price fixing; charges of conspiracy; lawsuits that have to be settled by the Department of Justice; authors taking out full-page ads railing against Amazon. It's hardly a dull industry. We care about what goes on in the book world because books are intimate objects. They inform the people we become by cracking open our world and making us understand things in new ways. In our younger years, many of us unlocked secrets and had the answers to some of life's most mysterious questions explained to us in the pages of books we were not supposed to be reading. When we love a book, we feel close to its author, even if it's in an intangible way. Celebrated authors are celebrities. Writers have power. They can expose wrongdoing, unveil secrets they were told to keep, change public opinion, and even affect the political process.

Today, many more people than ever before are becoming published authors. What used to be reserved for a select few change-makers and talented scribes is now accessible to anyone who chooses to publish. And while the ramifications of that will be something we'll explore in this book, the fact that anyone can publish a book has created a new publishing paradigm that is somewhat labyrinthine. The broader world of book publishing, encompassing all forms of publishing—traditional, hybrid, and self (which I will define in detail in this chapter)—touches everyone who reads and impacts everyone who writes and either is published or aspires to publish.

A whopping 300,000 books were traditionally published in 2014, and Bowker's most recent statistics (for 2013) count 458,564 self-published titles and growing. The volume of books in the marketplace, coupled with the fact that consumers (mostly) buy books online, is creating a free-market opportunity that's exciting for independent authors but terrifying for publishers, especially traditional publishers. Fewer books than ever before are selling six-digit numbers (even five-digit numbers, for that matter), because more inventory means more choice for consumers. Publishers that used to bank on a handful of books to break the one hundred thousand sales mark each year might still hope for that, but these kinds of performances are increasingly rare. And while there's a lot of talk about how digital technology—in the form of e-books—is changing the face of book publishing, it's not as big a game-changer as many people think. In 2014, e-book sales made up only about 20 percent of all book sales, a percentage that's remained relatively stagnant since 2010. In fact, the biggest thing affecting the book business these days is therefore not e-readers and e-books but rather more books—sheer volume. The publishing landscape, because so much is in flux, is still the Wild West, where anyone, no matter how they choose to publish, has the possibility to come out of the deal exceeding their wildest expectations. Yet the volume issue has also caused a new problem (or obsession, depending on how you look at it): discoverability. It's difficult to get discovered when there is so much competition. It's also difficult to get reviews and media attention and publicity hits. However, this is the world you set foot in when you choose to publish, so, rather than bemoaning how many other people are joining the ranks of published authors or wishing there were more readers than writers, you've got to suck it up and play ball.

Today's Paths to Publishing

Let's start here with a quick overview of what's what so that we're clear about today's publishing landscape and what options exist for writers who decide to pursue getting published. For those of you pretty clear on the differences between traditional publishing and self-publishing, it's fine to skip ahead, but I recommend taking a moment to browse through the myriad variations on hybrid publishing that exist. This is publishing's emerging middle ground, and it's the part of the industry most likely to explode in years to come, as traditional publishing's barriers get higher and higher and self-published authors, having experienced the limitations of self-publishing, move toward hybrid models themselves.

TRADITIONAL

Traditional publishing is the kind of publishing most people think of when they think about book publishing. This is where an author writes a manuscript, or a proposal and some sample chapters, and then shops their work to an agent or goes directly to a publisher. Most bigger publishers do not accept unsolicited manuscripts, which means that authors have to be agented to even get in the door. Many smaller publishers will work with authors directly, and for some very small publishers, an agent might be superfluous, particularly if there's no advance being offered.

Traditional publishers typically, but not always, pay an advance. In return, they keep the lion's share of the profit from the sales of your book. The industry standard is for traditional publishers to keep 85 percent of paperback net sales and 75 percent of e-book net sales. Traditional publishers almost always have an in-house marketing and publicity department dedicated to their lists. The amount of money and energy they allocate to your book depends on how they decide to position and prioritize it (see "Traditional Publishing's Courting Problem," below), and your ability to influence any decision making about your own book is largely out of your control.

Your publisher owns the rights to publish your book for the lifetime of your contract. You hold the copyright, as is the case with all publishing. The likelihood of your ever getting a second book deal with the same publisher or another publisher is wholly dependent on your first book's sales. If your book tanks, you may well become a pariah in the industry, an author no one will touch because of your poor track record. If your book does well, your publisher will be happy, and it won't be too long before they come knocking, asking what you're working on next. Traditional publishing in this sense is a lot like fashion: one day you're in, and the next day you're out.

HYBRID

Hybrid publishing is an emerging area that occupies the middle ground between traditional and self-publishing and therefore includes many different publishing models—basically anything that is not self-publishing or traditional publishing. "Hybrid publishing" is not a term all publishers or authors in this space use; other terms that describe this type of publishing include "author-assisted publishing," "independent publishing," "partnership publishing," "copublishing," and "entrepreneurial publishing." But right now, because it's a catchall, "hybrid publishing" is the umbrella term I'll use throughout this book to refer to this middle ground.

The hybrid publishing space is somewhat controversial, in part because it's new, and in part because there's no universal agreement about what it is. Because hybrid models almost always involve the author paying for some or all services (and always in return for higher royalty rates), some assert that hybrid publishing is the same as vanity publishing. For people who like to think in black-and-white terms, the hybrid publishing space upends their sense of order. Without hybrid, there are just traditional publishing and self-publishing. Black and white. You get paid to publish or you pay to get published. The hybrid publishing space is not for black-and-white thinkers. There are a number of models, and in my experience what sets them apart from vanity presses is that they're run like publishing companies. Many of them have a submissions process, control their own cover design and editorial process, and have publishers calling the shots and curating the lists. There are also traditional publishers that are cutting hybrid deals, in which authors pay for some services in exchange for higher royalties.

The payoff for the author in hybrid publishing comes from having more control. The author is investing in their own work, or perhaps raising money through crowdfunding to finance their work, and then keeping the lion's share of their profits, rather than giving it all away. Authors retain creative ownership and are treated more like partners in the process, instead of being at the whim of their publishers.

The following are four kinds of hybrids that I've identified as of the writing of this book:

1. Traditional publishers that have been brokering hybrid publishing deals for years.

The precedent for hybrid models goes back years and years. A number of publishers have cut deals with authors for what might have been qualified as "distribution deals," "hybrid publishing arrangements," or "copublishing ventures." All this means is that the author pays up front in some capacity. This might be for part or all of the print run or the cost of production. In exchange, the author usually negotiates a higher royalty rate, since they've invested in their own work. The only downside to this variation of hybrid publishing is that it's not transparent. Most of the traditional publishers who do it don't talk about it, because the concept of authors paying to publish is so heavily stigmatized. In fact, it's still the case that authors who subsidize any part of their work are barred from submitting their work to some reviewers and to many contests. These authors do not qualify for membership in certain writers' associations. (Thankfully, many review outlets, contests, and associations are changing their tune on this, but not enough of them and not fast enough.)

2. Partnership publishing models.

Models like these include my own publishing company, She Writes Press. Our authors absorb the financial risk of their publishing endeavor in exchange for high royalties. We offer traditional distribution (which we'll explore in detail in Chapter 6) and all the benefits that brings.

Partnership publishing models like She Writes Press are exciting in that they offer authors access—to review sites, to a sales force selling their books into the marketplace, and to a partnership with a publisher that has a strong reputation with booksellers. The downside, however, is that there's a real financial risk. Publishers mostly don't earn out their investments on books they acquire, and partnership publishing is no different. You are assuming the financial risk for access and for the possibility of a high reward. However, it's a competitive marketplace out there, and I always encourage authors to go into this option with their eyes wide open. It's not a foregone conclusion that your investment will be recouped. Other presses like ours include Ink Shares, Booktrope, BQB Publishing, and Turning Stone Press.

3. Agent-assisted publishing models.

Many agents are starting their own publishing companies in order to publish the works of authors whose books they cannot sell.

For the most part, these efforts are valiant. Agents feel strongly about the work they're seeing and want to find an outlet where these authors can be published. They're hybrid because the authors are being published under the agent's imprint. What these models lack to date is any kind of effective distribution method. Where they excel, and what makes them like the other two models above, is in understanding publishing and putting out quality books that their authors can be proud of. One asset here as well may be on the foreign-market side. If your agent continues to represent you and has published your book, it's likely they will make strong efforts to sell foreign editions of your work, so be sure to ask. Examples of agent-assisted publishing include Reputation Books (a division of Kimberley Cameron & Associates) and the Curtis Brown Group out of the UK.

4. Other assisted publishing models.

What makes assisted self-publishing models different from the partnership and agent-assisted models is that they may or may not be run by someone who knows about books. In these cases, you are paying someone to help you publish. You are not working with a team that is going to publish your work under their imprint. This model really qualifies more as self-publishing than as hybrid. However, I believe it's important to include these models here, more as a caution to aspiring authors than anything else. Just because you are working with a company does not mean that it is a good hybrid company with services that will help your book succeed. The market for book publishing has exploded, and as a result a number of companies have cropped up to deal with the pain points unique to authors—namely, that getting a book from manuscript to publication is a complicated process. Many of these companies have given the word "vanity" some propulsion because they're not vetting and they don't care about editorial quality. That's on the author, which is why I believe this is somewhat dangerous territory in which you need to be careful. This is basically expensive self-publishing, and some of these companies outright take advantage of authors. The company with the most notoriety in this space is Author Solutions (home of iUniverse, Balboa, WestBow Press, and Archway, to name a few). Not all assisted publishing models are bad, but some of them have a reputation for exploiting authors, so you want to be careful. Do your homework.

SELF-PUBLISHING

There are two ways to self-publish: assisted self-publishing and DIY self-publishing. With the former, you hire someone to guide you through the self-publishing process, while with the latter, you truly do it all yourself.

There is a lot at stake when you're self-publishing, and for that reason there are few instances in which I'd recommend going fully DIY. In fact, the only circumstance in which it's a good idea to go fully DIY is if you have serious editorial skills and design savvy and are certain you can navigate these territories on your own. Over the years, I've worked with a number of authors who've done DIY publishing, and the results have been mostly poor, almost always because of design—bad covers and badly executed interiors. The sad thing is that these authors generally have no idea that their books don't look good. People in the book world know a self-published book when they see one, and your exclusive goal as a self-published author is to ensure that your book does not look self-published, which is why I recommend working with someone who knows what they're doing. It's worth paying a consultant to guide you through the publishing process and worth hiring a person or a team who can offer you all the pieces—a copyedit, a proofread, cover design, interior design, e-pub conversion, and file setup and upload. This is not to say that a single consultant will have all these skill sets, but rather that they have a stable of people who work with them who can execute the many steps necessary to publish a book. Assisted self-publishing is basically turning over the editorial and production of your project to an expert who's done what you're wanting to do many times before.

If you want to learn how to self-publish truly on your own, you are going to undergo some growing pains that are a natural part of earning expertise, and as long as you are in it for the knowledge and the learning experience, DIY might be a perfect fit for you. But do yourself a huge favor and ask for professional opinions. Find a mentor you can bounce ideas off, and don't be obstinate or prideful if someone gives you negative feedback about either editorial or design. Get more feedback, and make the necessary course corrections. Your reputation hinges on it.

Shifting Your Publishing Perspective

Established traditional publishers who've been doing their thing for the better part of a century have not been quick to adapt to the changing marketplace. They've instead behaved a bit like children who stick their fingers in their ears and cover their eyes, hoping to wish a problem away by pretending it isn't there. The problem traditional publishers face is that their way of doing things doesn't make sense. They're still spending huge amounts of money for projects that have little hope of ever earning out the giant bidding price. There are fewer houses buying projects, but because they're operating the way they always have, they're stuck in a cycle where they show their faith in a project or an author by offering big advances. There's pressure to do so, too, from agents and from the houses themselves. It's a crazy system in which all parties involved—agents, authors, editors, and publishers—put their faith in a given book's success based on the dollar amount offered for it. This mentality is a holdover from a bygone era when there were many fewer books in the marketplace and when big-name authors could sell the kind of volume that would justify six-figure advances.

A handful of authors today still have the Midas touch, such a brand and a loyal readership that anything they write justifies the huge advances they get, but houses still throw six-figure advances at the next big thing—based on hype, on an agent's sway in the matter, and on auctions that escalate a book's value rapidly by using scarcity tactics and pitting publishers against one another.

In my first book, *What's Your Book?*, I concluded with a subsection called "The Future of Publishing." More than three years have passed, and my feelings about publishing are largely unchanged. I still believe it's a privilege to be published on a traditional press, but I also believe it's an option to pursue with a critical eye. My cofounder of She Writes Press, Kamy Wicoff, has described those for whom traditional publishing actually works as the 1 percent. These are the authors who get the big advances, the red-carpet treatment, and the kind of attention every author dreams of to make their books a real success. Their publishing houses will set them up to succeed by spending marketing dollars and creating a sizable plan that opens doors and creates opportunities. But for the other 99 percent, traditional publishers are offering a mixed bag. Yes, they're paying you to publish, or they're fronting the publishing bill without an advance, but too often they end their investment there and do little by way of marketing and publicity or engage in what's known as the spaghetti approach to marketing—throwing a bunch of noodles at the wall and hoping something sticks.

Book publishing is a complicated and fascinating industry, and it behooves authors of every stripe to understand it. Mostly I believe this because in so doing you set yourself free to explore your options and to truly embrace that traditional publishing is not the only way. If you're reading this book, you are probably not the 1 percent, and I don't say that to disparage or discourage you—quite the opposite, in fact. I want the 99 percent to fully embrace their publishing options, and to have the confidence even to reject a traditional deal if one that doesn't meet their needs comes their way. Among the 150-plus authors that have signed with She Writes Press as of the writing of this book, three turned down traditional publishing deals, and a number of them simply "opted out," deciding that the traditional route was going to be too time-consuming and too soul-sucking.

We have been on the edge of a new frontier in publishing for about the last decade, and there's no sign of the muddy waters clearing. The thing that matters most when it comes to publishing your work is that you're proud of what you're putting out into the world. The journey to get there will be wholly your own. You may shift your perspective because you feel open to possibilities and excited about the new publishing climate; you may be forced to shift your perspective because multiple rejections have left you disappointed. The path you take to get to a new way of thinking—whether it's been full of agency and wonder or a giant kick in the ass—is less important than how you feel once you arrive. Even if you feel somewhat resentful of the idea that you have to pay to publish your own work or deflated because the industry has not validated your writing the way you thought it would, you get to decide whether to be your own champion. When you green-light your work and do it with pride, the sky is the limit. If you do it with a sense that you're choosing the second-best option and approach the prospect of alternative publishing with a chip on your shoulder, I'm telling you now, you shouldn't even bother.

The Real Value of Publishing

Many authors I work with hold a view based on the golden age of publishing—the 1930s through '50s—when authors like F. Scott Fitzgerald, Ernest Hemingway, and Gertrude Stein had wonderful relationships with editors and houses who cultivated their talent for the long haul. This was long before the Internet and the concept of author as a brand. It was before Oprah and TED talks and before an author platform played a role in who got published or not.

I blog for the *Huffington Post*, and in response to something I wrote about the value of getting published, a reader wrote a comment saying he didn't believe that books now hold the kind of cultural value they once did. He wrote:

> "Books and literature no longer play [sic] an important place in our culture. Millions of people will never read a book for pleasure. The days when writers like Norman Mailer and Gore Vidal were guests on *The Johnny Carson Show* and were considered public intellectuals who were solicited for their opinions on current events [are] long gone."

I objected to this viewpoint because there's evidence to the contrary. Today's intellectuals may look a little different than the intellectuals of yesteryear. Today, instead of Mailer and Vidal, we have gurus like Eckhart Tolle and Brené Brown, who are household names for the words they've put into books. Consider books like *Quiet: The Power of Introverts in a World That Can't Stop Talking* and *Outliers: The Story of Success* and *Gulp: Adventures on the Alimentary Canal*. The authors of these books—Susan Cain, Malcolm Gladwell, and Mary Roach, respectively—are intellectuals spreading their wisdom to the masses through the books they write, and through speaking gigs, TED talks, webinars, and the pure generation of content (in the form of articles and new books).

Authors' words are still valued, and authors today make appearances on morning television shows, though those shows have got nothing on what a single endorsement from Oprah can still do, even in the years since her show went off the air. But it's not just national media that makes authors relevant today. Any writer with a message who's consistently engaging in conversation with their readers is contributing cultural value through their writing, and I'd argue that these kinds of gurus abound. Some of them have modest but loyal followings, and plenty of these "small-time" gurus are publishing their own work because they have to. These authors may have a loyal following of two thousand to five thousand people (nothing to sneeze at), but to the publishing industry, that's a pile of beans when the likes of Kris Carr and Gretchen Rubin, with their crazy-robust databases, and, even further up the celebrity ladder, Lea Michele, Gwyneth Paltrow, and Cameron Diaz, have all written books in the past couple of years. Yet my point is this: you do not have to be one of these supercelebs to be or become a go-to person who's solicited for your opinions. But you do have to have a book.

Because traditional publishing is contracting, mostly publishing only books whose authors bring an established brand, many writers are having to find alternative ways of being heard. This is where the rubber meets the road, and where alternative publishing starts to look very attractive. I've met countless bright, articulate leaders in their fields who cannot get traditional publishing deals. I've written extensively about how frustrating it is to see another *Duck Dynasty* book, or books authored by the likes of Kris Jenner and Bethenny Frankel, while authors doing groundbreaking work on small scales can't get publishing deals to save their lives. The same is true—even more so—for novelists and memoirists. In fact, one of the reasons I started She Writes Press was because of the quality of work I was rejecting during my tenure at Seal Press, the indie darling I referenced in the introduction. By the time the Seal acquisitions committee got to the point where author platform mattered more than the actual quality of the book, I had already all but given up.

The traditional publishing industry is no longer doing what it was founded to do: curate worthy books. In its heyday, traditional publishing was responsible for setting the tempo of our cultural conversation. Today many of us are dismayed by the direction the cultural conversation is going in. We are experiencing a cultural dumbing-down, and the traditional houses are contributing to it, rather than combating it—all in the name of the bottom line. Thankfully, the Big Five publishing houses (Penguin Random House, Macmillan, HarperCollins, Hachette and Simon & Schuster) are still publishing culturally and intellectually worthy books, but not consistently, and not across the board. That's why authors must take the reins, and why it's incredibly important that we as a culture embrace alternative forms of publishing. The publishing industry's no is not what it once was. You cannot begin to build the platform publishers want you to have without a book, but you won't get a book deal without the fan base. This is a frustrating catch-22 would-be authors face, for which green-lighting your own work is the only antidote.

Traditional Publishing's Courting Problem

When an acquiring editor at a publishing house decides they want to buy a book, they must court the author—selling their press and their own services to the prospective author they want to onboard. It's a lot of work for the editor who's doing the courting and quite flattering to the author who's being courted. In the selling, the editor (and sometimes the publisher and marketing team, too) is pulling out all the stops. During this time, editors are not always 100 percent honest about what will and will not happen once an author signs their contract. I know this because I found myself in this position countless times, drawing up marketing plans, making promises, taking authors out to fancy dinners. It's not that editors outright lie to the authors they're courting as much as that they aren't transparent about the efforts expected of the author, or how much money will actually be allocated to the author's publicity budget, or about the fact that the editor and publicity team have a whole host of other authors on the list and they're all vying for the attention of an in-house publicist or two.

Agents reinforce this lack of transparency by holding high expectations and fussing over their authors. More than a few agents during my years as an acquiring editor told me that their clients needed "more love." In other words, they needed me to stroke the authors' egos and tell them how amazing I thought their book was. I get it, believe me. What author wouldn't want their editor calling them up and telling them how amazing their book is? The problem for me was that I wanted to do this only if I authentically felt that way, and I often did not. Too many authors, as a result of the fussing and the courting, wanted to sit back and have work done for them—both on the editorial front and on the marketing front—and when the author stopped being an equal partner in the business venture, I felt at my wits' end. But hadn't we set up this dynamic?

Whether the author knows it or not, by the time they sign their publishing contract, the honeymoon period is over. It's short-lived because the acquiring editor is focused on making the deal. I'm sure some of you will argue that you had amazing relationships with your editors and that you've published multiple books at the same house. Perfect. That's likely because your book was an "A-list title." In other words, your book was chosen. Books are chosen for a number of reasons. Sometimes it's because of the writing. More often than not, however, it's about the author: who they are; their connections; their platform. After all, the author (in today's publishing climate) is what sells the book. Everyone else, the B's and C's who will never, ever know their status, is often scraping the bottom of the publisher's marketing and finance resource barrel.

The reason I call this a courting problem is because of the expectation that's set up and the very long fall for the author who can't understand what's happened once the relationship starts going south. They're blindsided because it all started out so well. They're the partner in the bad relationship who keeps wondering how something once so good is now so complicated. But after the courting is done, acquisitions editors are on to the next book. Some authors get little to no attention from their acquiring editor, in part because they have a quota to make. But authors don't see this, and they don't understand it. This is what I was talking about in the introduction when I said that publishing with a traditional house is a privilege that sometimes comes with strings attached. The publisher has paid you an advance and is paying for your publishing costs. So when they decide that you're not the most important author on their list, it feels weird—like, *Didn't you want me?* But if you're a B or C title, this is likely what your experience with your publisher is going to be like. You won't have the access you want, the relationship you hoped for, or the experience you dreamed of.

And because publishers have to fill lists, there are countless authors who have mediocre (at best) experiences with traditional publishing. Not surprisingly, many of those authors are opting out for their next books. They're seeing what's possible in the world of hybrid and self-publishing and choosing to make a go of it.

Traditional publishing has a problem on its hands because it's not going to be able to keep this up. It relies on those B's and C's *sometimes* to be breakout books. No one knows when a sleeper will hit. Oftentimes, the most successful books are the ones you wouldn't have bet the farm on. Maybe it's because the author is a rock star who doesn't pull out all her secret stops until postpublication; maybe it's because the topic or the story is the right thing at the right time. We're not there just yet, but there will come a tipping point when the 99 percent starts to see that publishers not only are not rolling out the red carpet but also are barely using what resources they have to push forward their own investment. I saw this personally when a well-published friend of mine had a book out with a major house. She'd published a couple of books before and finally got picked up by one of the Big Five. They paid a big advance for the book, and she had a good relationship with her editor. But then the book published, and it seemed like they were doing the bare minimum where her publicity efforts were concerned. As time wore on, it became clear that that was indeed the case. What happened here? Why did this publisher pay a six-figure advance and then do only the most basic outreach? I'm not inside this big house, but my sense is that another book or several books were getting better media attention than my friend's book and so that's where the resources went. The publisher chases the leads and abandons ship on projects that don't take off right away.

In traditional publishing, you are in fact competing against the other authors on your list. If the in-house publicist has two similar books to promote, she chooses which one to focus on.

There is sometimes not enough to go around. When my friend asked her publisher what was going on, the publisher shirked their responsibility. They were getting a lot of publicity, her editor said, but it wasn't "sticky." My friend tried to push for more. Her agent tried to push for more. But you're in a tough position with your publisher if they've decided to move on. You can ask for what you want—pressure for it, demand it—but if your publisher has decided they've done all they can for your book, you have no leverage. This is not your financial investment, after all; it's theirs. So you're pretty much out of luck.

Discrimination in Review Outlets, Contests, and Associations

Yes, discrimination might sound like a strong word, but that's exactly what's happening in publishing circles today. Publishing is a big moneymaker, and authors are happily forking over money to get published. Review outlets were quick to pick up on ways to monetize self-published authors' desire to be reviewed by creating separate "self-published only" reviews, like *Publishers Weekly*'s Select program and *Kirkus*'s Indie Reviews.

I've heard Jim Milliot, of *Publishers Weekly*, describe self-published authors as traditional publishing's farm team. This means that traditional publishing houses are looking to find the self-published standouts, to scoop them up and give them publishing deals. This is now a regular occurrence, in fact, as big houses have picked up originally self-published books—like *The Celestine Prophecy*, by James Redfield; *Still Alice*, by Lisa Genova; and *Fifty Shades of Grey*, by E. L. James—that have demonstrated success in their self-published iterations. Like baseball's farm team of guys who'd die for a chance to play in the big leagues, most authors would give anything to get published by a big house. But what this analogy promotes is the idea that self-published authors have not arrived and that they are somehow less-than. They have not made it to the big leagues, and they are still striving.

Traditional publishing has largely ghettoized the self-publishing community, and paid reviews are just another way of creating a divide. The fact that two separate tracks for getting reviews exist—one paid and one unpaid—says that traditional authors do not have to pay because they have been "chosen," while everyone else has not been. They have not been given the keys; they do not have the access. This permeates other spheres of publishing, as I referenced earlier, specifically contests and associations. There are a number of contests—among them the Ohioana Annual Book Awards, the Phillip H. McMath Post-Publication Book Awards, the Permafrost Book Prize in Nonfiction, and the Commonwealth Club's California Book Awards—whose rules stipulate that author-subsidized projects are not welcome. Some associations, notably Mystery Writers of America and International Thriller Writers, close their doors to self-published authors. Even the Authors Guild, whose mission is to support working authors, allows membership only to authors who've earned at least $5,000 on their writing over the previous eighteen months. It's a particularly interesting angle, because they set an arbitrary bar, since there's no need to provide receipts showing what a given author might have spent on publicity, for instance, while shutting their doors to authors who are not making money at their writing. Most authors I know, even the traditionally published ones, are spending money and reinvesting in themselves as writers. We will talk about the problems inherent in a world where only those who can afford to publish can publish. However, this kind of elitism within the industry should be named for what it is. It says that if a publisher at a major house has not deemed your work worthy, you are not worthy of receiving a fair review, of entering your work into a contest to be judged (fairly, one would hope, on the merit of the work), or of being a member of an association that is about writing, not (ostensibly) about who publishes you or whether you got paid to publish. Thankfully, some organizations, like the Historical Novel Society and Romance Writers of America (RWA), do open their membership to all authors. RWA's site stipulates that authors must be "seriously pursuing a career in romance fiction." This is a much more refreshing criterion than how much money said authors may or may not be earning on their work. After all, we all have to start somewhere, and many authors are not earning significantly on their books until they have a number of books in print.

If traditional publishing were holding up a high standard with every book published, I might tone down my firm accusations of wrongdoing here, but because they are publishing many books whose literary merit is questionable at best, we need to take a hard look at these review sites, contests, and associations and demand equality. In a country fighting so many battles against discrimination, this is another thing to add to the pile. But it's important that authors who've paid their way not lie down and take it just because the discriminatory rules reaffirm some sense of their not having "made it."

When you green-light your own work, you have made it. You are brave for having confidence enough in your own work to endorse it, to look at what's happening in the world around us, and to say, *I deserve to be published. My work is worthy.* It's necessary to note here that the authors I work with who greenlight their own work are always well edited. They are vetted by editors, readers, and sometimes publishers and acquiring editors at houses who write positive rejection letters telling them that they adored their manuscript but couldn't acquire it for any number of reasons, ranging from lack of platform to a house's having recently published a similar book.

I implore you to stand up against this kind of discrimination when and where you encounter it. Organizations like the Independent Book Publishers Association are already taking strides in their author advocacy to bring issues like these to the forefront, but the only way to level the playing field and to eradicate discrimination in publishing circles is to name it when you see it. Write letters to the review outlets, contests, and associations. Include your endorsements, awards you may have won, and any other accolades in your signature line, or in the body of the letter itself. The only way to change the industry is to force the insiders who are setting these rules to see that what matters is not whether an author pays for their work. What matters is the work itself, and that stands on its own, regardless of an author's path to publishing.

Chapter 2.

The Indie Revolution and Your Role in It

When I left traditional publishing in 2012, I was of the opinion that independent publishing was a term reserved for traditional publishers. I'd worked for "independent publishers" for years—and the term, to me, distinguished independently owned presses from corporate publishing houses. Having spent the years since immersed in the nontraditional side of publishing, I see that today when people talk about "indie" authors, they're talking not about authors published on small presses but about a thriving movement of self-published authors and authors who finance their own book projects. The term "indie" celebrates a certain spirit—of independence, obviously, but also of not needing affiliation or approval or not needing to operate within the parameters of the existing paradigm. These are the authors who are green-lighting their own work, and they're riding the wave of a movement that's far from peaking. In a 2014 Forbes.com article, "Indies: How Your Next-Door Neighbor Is Changing Commerce," David Vinjamuri called the larger movement of indie craftspeople and artisans creating and selling their own products the Indie Revolution. Authors creating and selling their own books are right at the heart of this movement.

As I said at the end of the last chapter, each of us has a different journey that lands us at the doorway where we will make the decision whether or not to green-light our book. But once you decide to do it, you're entering the company of many who've come before you, and it's an exciting place to be. The Indie Revolution that Vinjamuri writes about includes people selling their fashion, crafts, and other wares at street fairs and trade shows, and on Etsy.com, as well as musicians, gamers, filmmakers, and, of course, authors. He differentiates indie from entrepreneur by noting the difference in these two groups' goals:

> The difference of mind has to do with the goals of entrepreneur versus the indie. The entrepreneur seeks control as a means to implementing a vision, where the vision is building an enterprise that can be sold or go public. In other words, the entrepreneur imagines a lifecycle that ends with control passing to others. The indie seeks the opposite, and often trades security and remuneration for independence and creative control.

A simple way to think about this is that entrepreneurs are looking to create a business, with profit as the bottom line. And while many authors enter publishing with the bottom line in mind, it's rarely the driving force behind their endeavors. Creativity, passion, and creative control are all bigger priorities than profit for most independently published authors. Authors will give up a lot to retain control, especially those authors who've had negative experiences as a result of not being in control of the publishing process, something some publishers seek to fully withhold from authors. Authors resent it when publishers who believe they know what's best for a book, regardless of what its creator might think, hold their creative projects hostage. I've heard too many horror stories to count about books that were mishandled and left the author feeling as if they'd compromised or, in extreme cases, as if the book no longer even felt like their own.

Publishing houses have long bred a culture of in-house secrecy, in that they seem to have a vested interest in not letting authors know what's going on. It's unclear where this tendency stems from or why this is the legacy of book publishing; perhaps it's so publishers can protect themselves, or perhaps it's an effort to remind the authors that the publisher ultimately holds the control and the power. This chapter explores and celebrates taking back that power by showcasing some examples of authors who've taken things into their own hands, some proactively and some because they believed they had no other option. There is no single silver-bullet publishing solution, but the fact that independent publishing is thriving and offering authors so many choices means that there's more to educate yourself about and more to investigate and explore. Figuring out where you land in this revolution may take some time. But as an indie author, you're a bit like a free agent—free to go where you choose—and that's an exciting thing once it stops being scary.

This is my fourth independently published book. I am one of those authors who never set foot on the traditional path and never will. By the time I decided to publish, I had my own press, for one, but I'd also grown cynical about what the publishing industry could do for an author like me, even if I had been able to eke out a very small deal for my niche book and my modest author platform. There were other things that deterred me from a traditional path, however: I didn't want to wait a year or two to publish, and I didn't want an in-house editor telling me what I could or could not write. Instead, I work with an editor on my own terms, one I trust and whom I've known for years, who will question my assertions when they're not well articulated and who will push me to write better. I work with a cover designer and trust her enough to know that she knows more than I do, but I get to say what I like and don't like and give her some direction about my preferences and vision. For me, green-lighting my own work is aligned with my values. Whether I don't crave the industry's stamp of approval because I've been in it and therefore know that the true value of that approval is meaningless or because of my personality—because I am happy to play in my own sandbox and appreciate creative control over outside validation—who knows? All that really matters is the fact that there are thousands like me, and we're part of this Indie Revolution together. If you're already with us, then you know it's exciting and bold and creatively challenging. And if you're on the edge of it looking in and you're curious and ready to see what it's all about, then read on.

What It Means to Be "Indie"

The term "indie," which is short for "independent," comes from the film and music world. To be indie has traditionally meant simply that an artist is not under contract, that they don't belong to a major studio or to a label. In publishing, indie presses were originally presses operated by an individual or individuals. They were called independent to differentiate themselves from corporate.

But the sands have been shifting for some years now, and this indie movement Vinjamuri writes about has been organizing itself for years, subtly but powerfully, and embedded in what it stands for are the values of an entire generation. It's clear from where I sit, as a younger member of Generation X, that some of this shift has to do with how Gen Xers (born between 1960 and 1980) and millennials (born between 1980 and 2000) have been raised. Largely, we want to work for ourselves. There's more creativity, more money to be made more quickly (in the sense that you don't necessarily have to work your way up), and more possibility for self-expression. Many, like I did, put in good years working for others, learning the ropes and figuring out how things work, before branching out on our own—often taking what we've learned and putting our own spin on it. The appetite among consumers for innovative ways of doing things is vast, and despite the initiative, resolve, and risk taking involved in entering this space, there seem only to be signs of growth in these independent movements. According to Vinjamuri's article, in 2013 on Etsy.com alone, "indie craftspeople and artisans ran over 1 million active shops (listing 25 million products) that sold $1.35 billion dollars of merchandise."

If you're part of the indie revolution, you're most likely straddling your indie passion with a full-time job, as many people are doing. Some of you will take the leap to pursue your indie passion full-time, while others will cobble together various ways to make a living—like Kirstin Jackson, author of *It's Not You, It's Brie: Unwrapping America's Unique Culture of Cheese*, who works as a cheesemonger at Solano Cellars in Berkeley, California, but also makes her own cheese, travels often to Europe to consult about cheese, works as a cheese consultant to local restaurateurs, and blogs on It'sAllAbouttheBrie.com. Her path is not uncommon, and she's an example of someone who's used her book to supplement and leverage the various things she does—and yet all of it is contained within a very specific area of expertise.

Those who do leave their day job to pursue their indie passions throw themselves into a brave new world of entrepreneurialism. Vinjamuri's distinction between an indie and an entrepreneurial mindset is well articulated, but there are of course those who embrace both—authors who embody indie values but who very much want to make money and scale their businesses, and who see book publishing as one piece of a larger pie that makes up the business of being an author.

In my experience with authors, I've seen that going indie starts with embracing passion. This is the thing that will get you out the gate and excited about what you're doing. But the most successful authors I work with are those who spend the time to understand the business side of things. They have a goal to earn out their expenses first, then to turn a profit. For most authors, this goal alone is ambitious, depending on the amount of money going into the project. It's typical for first-time authors not to earn out their expenses, but if publishing is coupled with a long-term vision that includes writing more books, developing expertise in your field, becoming a consultant or a teacher, growing your existing business, and/or getting speaking engagements and other kinds of gigs, then it behooves you to look at your book as a vehicle that will open doors and that, by extension, gives you a platform for your message, ideas, and/or creativity.

One of the keys to true indie success is to embrace it fully. A lot of authors out there are quietly publishing their books and going about their business. Maybe they don't want people to know that they self-financed. Maybe publishing their book was just something to tick off their to-do list. Maybe they're struggling with their own judgments about what they're doing. I had a client, Sandy, whose writing was dragging. She could not, for the life of her, write more than maybe one thousand words per week. She would show up to our sessions often deflated, telling me that her family didn't "let her write." Her husband and two adult children were always hijacking her time. She had left a job in finance to pursue a later-in-life and new career as a psychic, and writing was supposed to be a part of that. Writing her book was going to support her business—bring her more clients and legitimize her work as a psychic to her husband. But she just couldn't do it, and eventually she wanted to discontinue our work together.

What I think happened was that Sandy couldn't legitimize her work to herself. She had left a big and important career to take this huge leap into the unknown. She had judgments about being a psychic, even though she was passionate about the work. She had grown up in a religious family, and her husband was conservative and didn't understand Sandy's "obsession," as he called it, with "woo-woo stuff." This perception was detrimental to Sandy, needless to say, but it also meant that shame was getting in the way of her ability to articulate her message. In the end, she was not in a place to embrace her DIY spirit, or to spread her message or write the book she felt called to write.

By contrast, another client of mine entered into a new business enterprise like a firecracker, full of ideas and enthusiasm for a new partnership she'd launched with an illustrator. Together, this writer-illustrator team, Norine Dworkin-McDaniel and Jessica Ziegler, envisioned a funny parenting site called Science of Parent hood.com, partnering illustrations with funny, quippy anecdotes and truisms about parenthood. This dynamic duo had their eye on the endgame from the moment they started working together. They focused on their platform and made an immediate name for themselves in the blogosphere with good content and high-level engagement with their audience. They did their research and decided they wanted to publish independently, and they fully embraced the spirit of the indie movement in everything they did. They were doing it all on their own—with good taste, high expectations for themselves, and persistence. They ultimately settled on publishing with She Writes Press, and they retained full creative control along the way. A year later (November 2015), their gorgeous book, *Science of Parenthood*, was out in the world. These coauthors never wavered, never felt guilty, never let anyone stand in their way. Theirs is a book that sings off the page and that was launched with a long-term vision in mind. I have no doubt these two have an amazing journey ahead of them, and *Science of Parenthood* is just the beginning.

Working Toward the Same Goal

Having worked with authors on both the traditional and the indie front, I know one thing to be true: we all have the same aspirations. We want to be validated, and we want people to read and love our books. Some feel a stronger pull toward money and fame than others, but those goals are largely secondary. In today's publishing climate, the thing that sets these two groups apart, of course, is that one subset has been "chosen" by the act of having been offered a publishing deal and the other subset has not. However, not all authors who are publishing independently have been rejected. Quite the contrary. More authors are choosing to self-publish as a first option and never even embark upon the traditional path.

Barbara Freethy is one such author, who was traditionally published and chose to self-publish her own backlist of books that had gone out of print—with great success. Another is Phil Cousineau, who shares with audiences that he publishes "one for me, and one for The Man." As a successful traditionally published author, Cousineau has seen how some of his projects are appealing to certain houses, while others—even some of which have more literary and cultural merit to him—are not. He is an example of a "hybrid author," someone who publishes both traditionally and nontraditionally. Increasingly more authors are opting to publish independently because they can see the limited scope of traditional publishers, and because their own definition of the success of a given book may not equal the many thousands of books a traditional publisher would have to sell to consider the book "not a failure" (never mind a success).

And while many more self-published authors have gone on to self-publish having faced rejection from traditional channels, they're seeing the cracks in the traditional paradigm enough to get to a place of acceptance around having chosen an alternative path, if not fully embracing it. Claire Cook, whose impressive publishing credentials you can find on Wikipedia, wrote a widely read post on Jane Friedman's blog called "Why I Left My Mighty Agency and New York Publishers (For Now)," in which she talked candidly about her experience of choosing to self-publish her latest novel, *Never Too Late*. She described how let down by traditional publishing she felt, and her decision not to let publishers break her heart and to instead take her book's future into her own hands. Another author with a similar story is Allison Winn Scotch, who self-published *The Theory of Opposites* after four books with traditional publishers. In an interview with *Parade* magazine, Winn Scotch said, in response to a question about what made her decide to self-publish:

> "For the past few years, I've watched a lot of really wonderful writers not be published correctly. . . . [I]t feels like, even though the book market has changed, the traditional publishers have not kept up with it. That's resulted in a lot of really discouraging experiences for authors, where their books are published, but nothing's really done by the publisher to sell them. And then the author's blamed for the numbers—or lack thereof. . . . But all of that said, I had a really lovely experience with the traditionals, really until my last book, where a lot of things felt like they went wrong that weren't in my control—including my editor leaving before my book came out. That really shifts the winds on how a book is pushed forward—and that's the third time that it happened to me in four books."

Needless to say, Winn Scotch took full control of *The Theory of Opposites*, and shortly after its release, actress Jennifer

Garner bought the film rights—so perhaps we'll see it as a movie on the big screen sometime soon.

Authors like Freethy, Cousineau, Cook, and Winn Scotch are trailblazers in that they're modeling a different way of thinking about publishing and rejecting the stigma that surrounds self-publishing as a lesser choice by saying, *I choose this*. These are celebrated authors whose work and books can be held up as the gold standard, and they can proudly claim that they did it right, retaining control and understanding the value of surrounding themselves with a good team of people to help them to the finish line.

In his 2013 acceptance speech for the Indie Champion Award, John Green, author of *The Fault in Our Stars*, said, in response to a question about whether he'd ever self-publish:

> "We must strike down the insidious lie that a book is the creation of an individual soul labouring in isolation. We must strike it down because it threatens the overall quality and breadth of American literature."

Later in this same speech, he said that authors "need editors and we need publishers and we need booksellers." This is an example of the black-and-white thinking I referenced in Chapter 1; it highlights a strong impulse some people have to categorize publishing into two camps, either/or. Green's comments suggest that traditional publishing is where things are done right, where authors have editors and get their books sold. Apparently, his vision of self-publishing is a process in which editing doesn't happen and books are not sold. In fact, it's not this way at all, and hybrid publishing is turning this notion completely on its head by offering independent authors access to a publisher and sales reps and booksellers. Furthermore, some traditional publishers are publishing books that could have used an additional editorial pass and whose covers are mediocre or just plain ugly, and plenty of self-published authors get themselves the much-needed editorial, design, and marketing support necessary to launch their books well and even get them into booksellers' hands. At the end of the day, it's about the author and their team. A traditionally published author can get lucky and have an amazing team with whom she sees eye to eye on every decision—or not. A self-published author can put together a rock star team to help him succeed, with whom he collaborates and brainstorms—or not.

Another important reminder to any author, evidenced by some of the stories shared here, is that publishing is fickle, and just because you sold one book and did well doesn't mean your next book is a shoo-in. You may find yourself on top of the world, with an editor you love, and she may leave, and there goes your champion. This is why it's always important to be open to whatever might come your way, and to consider that even ten years from now you might be surprised to find yourself self-publishing your own backlist. You never know. If you're a self-published author, maybe you'll get scooped up by a traditional house because you published your book so darn well; if you're a traditionally published author, maybe your house won't pick up your next book and you'll decide to take a stab at hybrid; if you're a hybrid author, maybe your next go-round will be self-publishing because you're interested in exploring the differences between the two models. Maybe by the end of your publishing journey you'll have had a hand in all three paths to publishing. *Viva la revolución.*

Time to Get Entrepreneurial

If you're reading this book because you want to publish one book and do it well, this next section is less pertinent than it is for those of you who want (or think you want) a writing career. Lots of people have aspirations about becoming authors and making money at writing, but most first-time authors often aren't quite geared up enough for what the long road of being in the business of writing actually looks like. The truth is that very few authors will make any significant headway with their first book—either in terms of readership or financially. Books still break out, but not in the way they once did. Because of the sheer volume of books being published that I spoke of in Chapter 1, publishers can no longer rely on those few stratospheric best sellers to carry their lists as they once did. Publishing strategist and former publisher Richard Nash explained this well in a 2013 *Poets & Writers* interview, in which he said:

> Given the dramatic increase in the total amount of content available, and the velocity at which it travels, we're seeing a shift from a world of a few handfuls of million-copy sellers and tens of thousands that sell four figures in units, to one where there is one series every two years that will sell ten million–plus, and millions that sell hundreds, or tens, or ones. In other words, the distribution of success has become even more skewed.

But there are things you can do to increase your chances, both of exposure and of having a long-term career as a writer. The first thing you want to do is start thinking about what your next book is going to be, even before your first book gets published. I've worked with a lot of authors who balk at this idea. They've spent ten years writing the book they've just finished, and they want a break. Or, they wonder, how are they supposed to work on building their readership, platform, marketing, and publicity and be writing a new book? But this is what career writers are doing. They are writing—a lot. And they're not just writing second books. They're blogging, contributing, and creating content on a weekly basis. There is no rest for the weary author who wants to succeed in today's incredibly competitive publishing climate.

Another thing you want to be thinking about at this stage, as you're finishing your first book and definitely before you gear up for a second, is to actually become a small business. Open a separate bank account for your writing business. It doesn't matter if there's no money coming in yet. Seed the bank account with $100 or whatever it takes to open a new account. If you have a full-time job, which most new writers do, then your writing will become a second job, if it's not already. If you already run your own business, then your writing will become a second business, not necessarily an extension of your first. Ideally, you will establish your writing business as an entity, an LLC or a corporation (check with a CPA or entity expert about which one makes the most sense for you), though making yourself a sole proprietor with a DBA is a sufficient way to start. While there are many good financial and tax reasons to make your business an entity (see sidebar), the biggest gain for you will be in legitimizing your "hobby." Setting yourself up as a business and adopting a businesslike mentality about your writing will encourage both you and others to take your writing a heck of a lot more seriously.

Advantages of Forming an LLC

by LG O'Connor

This invaluable information is reprinted by permission of its author, LG O'Connor, and can be found on her blog at www.lgoconnor.com.

PERSONAL ASSET PROTECTION: Exactly what the name implies, an LLC provides for limited liability and protects your personal assets in the case of a lawsuit. Think nothing can happen to you? I'm sure *American Sniper*'s Chris Kyle thought so, too. Jesse Ventura won a defamation suit against his estate. Lucky for him, HarperCollins shared the burden as part of their libel insurance, but for small-time authors? Not happening. If you are a published author, I hope you've read the fine print on your publishing contracts around liability and had a good lawyer make the necessary modifications. The standard contract language will push the burden onto the author.

For this reason, I sign all my contracts—and publish—under my LLC, not as an individual.

TAX BENEFITS: When I hit the total key on all my business-related expenses for last year, I almost fainted. No surprise, the business ran at a loss for the second year in a row. People sometimes try to write off expenses without forming a company, but, according to my accountant, where they run the risk of an audit and being considered a "hobbyist" is when they

(continued on next page)

commingle funds in a personal bank account. It's essential to set up a separate business account for paying business-related expenses.

So here comes the benefit. Depending on your financial situation, writing off your expenses can do one of two things: 1) help you get a refund, or 2) reduce your tax bill. This year, I reduced my taxes—not by hundreds, but by *thousands*. My 2014 tax benefit exceeded my book sales by roughly 300 percent—meaning I would've magically had to come up with thousands of dollars by April 15 had I not had a business to write them off against.

TAX IMPLICATIONS OF HAND-SOLD BOOKS VS. SELLING BOOKS THROUGH YOUR PUBLISHER: Beware of this little tax implication. Royalties are taxed using *Schedule E*, while hand-sold books are taxed using *Schedule C*. What's the difference? Books you sell yourself are considered merchandise, and, in addition to state sales tax, they are subject to self-employment tax.

Your obligations as an LLC

There are four obligations that I have as a sole proprietor LLC in my state:

1. I have to file an annual report online and pay a $50 fee. (In California, this fee is to the State Franchise Board, and it's $800. Note that the fee will vary by state, but the savings are still enough to offset the annual payment.) The state will send you a reminder in the mail well in advance of your anniversary.

2. By January 31 every year, I must issue individual 1099-MISCs to any vendor/service provider to whom I've paid $600 or more during that tax year (i.e., editors, cover designers, formatters, etc.). You'll need their tax number, name, and address. No need to file if their business is a designated corporation.

3. By February 28 every year, I must also file a 1096 to the government with a list of my 1099-MISC recipients. My accountant prepares both my 1099-MISCs and my 1096. All I have to do is sign and send them in. You have longer to file if done electronically.

4. Quarterly: submit sales and use tax online, even if my sales were $0 for the quarter. Takes five minutes.

As I said earlier, being indie- and entrepreneurially minded are not necessarily mutually exclusive, and in order to succeed at this business of writing, you have to constantly be on the lookout, brainstorming and acting on how to take the material you have and grow it, morph it, and repurpose it. I've come across certain businesspeople in my career whose entire business model has to do with creating products from content. It takes tons of work to tease your content into various forms and products and therefore falls into a whole different subset—entrepreneurialism on steroids—that seems to work particularly well for authors of nonfiction work.

An example of a person who's doing this work out in the world in an active way is John C. Robinson, founder of Passion-

Quest Technologies and best-selling author. His passion for bird-watching led first to a book on the subject. From there, he immediately saw ways to leverage this into multiple products, which included teaching, audio products, spin-off books, workbooks, and eventually tours. With one book, he's claimed to have created upwards of thirty products, and now he teaches other authors how to do what he's done—repurpose content into products that will bring multiple streams of income. For some authors, this kind of financial orientation to their content is exciting. It can feel limitless, and indeed it can be—especially if you have the right niche content to make this kind of leveraging work.

In the fiction world, we're seeing genre fiction authors take the self-publishing world by storm with a model that involves writing a book a year (if they're not on an even more rigorous schedule). Genre fiction refers to any kind of fiction in a subgenre—like science fiction, fantasy, romance, erotica, thrillers, horror, etc. This kind of output has been happening for years with authors like Dean R. Koontz (in horror) and Danielle Steel (in romance). Among today's superstar self-published authors in this space are Hugh Howey, Amanda Hocking, and Michael J. Sullivan. What this new crop of genre writers has discovered is that there seems to be a limitless appetite for story, and the best way to get known (and therefore to make money) is to produce, produce, produce.

At the end of the day, being an entrepreneurial writer requires a shift in attitude that can be a game-changer. Too often, people's writing is relegated to insignificance, either by writers themselves or by their partner or their parents. The conditioning we get around "writing as hobby" starts young. If you pursued a liberal-arts major in college, you're in the minority if someone in your life didn't tell you that you weren't going to be able to support yourself with a degree like that. Many writers have fantasies of supporting themselves with their writing but understand that it's just that—a fantasy. If it were to happen someday, great, but in the meantime, they'll keep their day job. I'm not saying you should quit your day job if you're not independently wealthy, but that doesn't mean you can't take tangible, daily steps to ensure you're taken seriously as a writer. If you dismiss it as something secondary, so will others. If you're willing to cancel or reschedule your writing time on a whim, then you're training the people in your life to believe that your writing is flexible and not a high priority. If you sit down to write and aren't in the mood, and don't try to get something on paper, then you're not treating your writing like work. Anyone with a job knows that some days (most days), you have to work even if you're not feeling it. Writing is the same. Set up your writing as a business, and treat it for what it is. If you happen to love what you do, lucky you. But don't do only what you love. That's not enough.

Money Talk

Not surprisingly, writers are not always motivated to write for money. A 2014 survey put out by Digital Book World and *Writer's Digest* discovered that the reasons writers write are in fact very nuanced. In this poll, which asked writers to rank the reasons why they write, "to make money writing books" ranked fourth, after 1) "to publish a book that people will buy," 2) "to build my career as a book writer," and 3) "to share my story with others."

In my own work, I encounter very few people who would stop writing if they knew that they had no hope of making any money on their writing. In fact, one of the questions I ask writers when they engage me for coaching is whether they intend to publish their work regardless of whether they get a traditional book deal. Roughly 95 percent of the people I speak to answer yes to this question. To the other 5 percent, I am honest and say that traditional deals are very hard to come by. And while most authors are still dreaming of a traditional publishing contract, the idea of not getting one is by no means the deterrent it once was.

But, yes, self-publishing or hybrid publishing means paying to get published, rather than having someone pay you to publish. Thinking about paying to be published requires authors to adopt a completely different mindset. For some, it's the death of a dream. For others, paying to publish is virtually impossible. They don't have the money, and they're never going to. Because I created a press whose model requires authors to invest in themselves up front, I've given a lot of thought to the money conundrum, and while I don't think I have any great solutions, I would be remiss not to give this topic some significant attention.

Some people can solve the money problem by deciding that they're going to shift their money values. Some people do have the money but can't wrap their mind around spending it on something that they always believed they would—or should—get paid to do. For others, it involves getting their family—i.e., the people who support them—on board with the idea that their work is valuable enough to invest money in. I've been at this long enough to understand how sticky money can get and also to know that "I don't have the money for that" isn't always a totally true statement.

Others, meanwhile, really do not have the money. They live on a fixed income; they make minimum wage; there's just no way. For these authors, I always suggest crowdfunding (which we'll discuss in more detail later in this chapter) as one option, at which some people bite and some people balk. I also suggest that they toil away on both their writing and their platform to build themselves up to a place where a publisher might take them on. I've known a lot of persistent authors who kept trying and trying and trying until they finally landed a publisher that covered their publishing expenses, even if they didn't pay an advance. There are also a number of publishing contests every year, and while these can feel like long shots, you absolutely must enter!

It's possible, too, for writers to publish an e-book for very little money, and to self-publish a print book, and do it well, for as little as $1,000–$1,500 if you're willing to learn a lot of things yourself. Joel Friedlander, at TheBookDesigner.com, offers authors resources (and free templates) for how to design their own book interior. Sites like 99designs.com offer book covers for $99. This is not typically the route I suggest authors take. It's certainly not a first choice, and the likelihood of ending up with a final product that is less than the gold standard is high. That said, if it comes down to publishing or not publishing, I always say to go with publishing. Say yes, because you will learn something about the process and about yourself. You will also gain readers. To my earlier point about the catch-22 of publishing, you're very unlikely to grow your platform if you don't have content, and there comes a point when blogging and social media posts aren't enough. An e-book can be a viable first step toward print publication.

For any author who tells me they cannot afford to create an e-book, I say yes, you can. Get a big mason jar and stick $5 a week in there for a year, and you will end up with $260. It is actually possible to create a good e-book for $260, if you have more time than money to research and self-educate. If you have a passion and a big enough dream, you will become a published author, and an e-book counts as being published. You'll be on Amazon, you'll get an Author Central profile, you'll sell books, you'll build a readership. It's all out there, waiting for you to go get it.

On a final financial note, it's important to remember that publishing your work is an investment in yourself and is not a wholly losing enterprise. You are putting money in for the eventuality of getting at least some of it back. I work with plenty of self-published and hybrid-published authors who have earned back their investments. A number of them have turned a profit. Very few are getting rich off their endeavors, but I know a handful of those authors, too. Investing in your own book is not sinking your hard-earned wages into a money pit; it's creating a salable product that has earning potential and that will legitimize you, put you on the map, and turn you into a go-to person on your subject matter. It's a door-opener and a thousand times more effective than a business card. It's scary to plunk down a whole bunch of dough for something that has an uncertain payoff, but there is growth and earning potential on the other side of this endeavor, and you must also measure these considerations as you decide whether to bank on yourself.

Crowdfunding

Crowdfunding is popular among authors who are looking to raise money to supplement their publication efforts, but it's not only about raising money. It's also a way to gain visibility for your book before you launch, in that it gives you a reason to rally people together around a cause or an idea. Many books are the seeds of movements, as in the case of titles like *Half the Sky: Turning Oppression into Opportunity for Women Worldwide*, by Nicholas Kristof and Sheryl WuDunn, a call to action to help women in developing countries impacted by sexual violence and sex trafficking, with a focus on microloans and girls' education as a real solution; or any of Michael Pollan's books about food, in which he touts the value of back-to-the-land eating. In *In Defense of Food*, Pollan's entire dietary premise is built on seven words: "Eat food. Not too much. Mostly plants." You don't have to have a manifesto in order to inspire people to donate. I've given money to Kickstarter campaigns when the work has touched upon something I believe in, like a children's book that depicted a transsexual parent and celebrated diversity.

Dorit Sasson, author of *Accidental Soldier: A Memoir of Service and Sacrifice in the Israel Defense Forces*, launched a crowdfunding campaign to raise money to support her publication goals with She Writes Press. What Sasson took away from the experience, she said, was that "crowdfunding is not for sissies." She ran a sixty-five-day campaign and set an ambitious goal to raise $20,000. In the end, she raised $2,454. Sasson does not consider her effort a failure, however. "Documenting the

(continued on next page)

experience, like I've done with my writing and editing process, has been invaluable, and a lot of support came in that way from other bloggers," she said. For Sasson, the sixty-five days were grueling, however, and took an emotional toll on her—which resulted in a much-needed vacation after it was all over.

For authors looking to try crowdfunding, you need to start by deciding whether to do all or nothing or to keep what you raise. If you opt for the latter, you generally pay a higher kickback to the platform for not having met your goal. The common wisdom among people who run a lot of crowdfunding campaigns is that the all-or-nothing option is the more effective one because there's more at stake—both for you and for the funders. It becomes a little more interesting for the funders involved to see whether you'll meet your goal, and it forces you to be realistic about your expectations when you set your fundraising goal right out of the gate.

Sarah Towle (sarahtowle.com) launched a successful Kickstarter campaign to finance the debut title of her multi-format publishing company, Time Traveler Tours & Tales. In addition to raising funds, Sarah wished to introduce her audience to her baseline concept of story-driven mobile tours to historic locations, which she'd then republish as interactive, e-, print, and audio books. Her crowd pledged $41,495 in support of producing *In the Footsteps of Giants,* by Mary Hoffman, as an interactive tour to Renaissance Florence. Sarah also banked on a successful campaign raising visibility for the effort, for the purpose of attracting potential investors. She is now consulting and teaching about crowdfunding and has the following ten tips for anyone interested in doing a crowdfunding campaign:

TIP 1: Do your research and choose your model and platform wisely.

TIP 2: Start building your campaign page right away.

TIP 3: Invite participation prelaunch—get your tribe involved and committed to pledge so that you know how much money you might confidently raise in week one.

TIP 4: Calculate your campaign goal based on the 80/20 rule—80 percent of those campaigns that raise 20 percent in their first week go on to fund.

TIP 5: Create a compelling campaign video.

TIP 6: Think hard about your rewards, and be realistic about their cost.

TIP 7: Communicate to your audience regularly, but in sound bites.

TIP 8: Thirty days is sufficient.

TIP 9: Preplan your promotions.

TIP 10: Stay present post-campaign; fulfill your promises.

I'd recommend attending a crowdfunding webinar and learning about the process so that you're well prepared for the endeavor. By all accounts, it's tough. It's emotionally taxing and requires you to reach deep inside yourself to keep promoting, motivating, and talking about your project and your goals. You want to make sure you're connecting to your audience in a heartfelt way and that you're clear about what they're getting in exchange for supporting you. This requires much planning and execution in advance, not while the campaign is under way, so make sure to give yourself plenty of prep time, and good luck!

Own It!

Owning your indie status is important, not just because when you do, you're embracing your spirit of independence, but also because of the ways in which being proud and able to articulate your "indie-ness" are aligned with the concept of green-lighting your work. When you're indie, you will not be tied down by other people's opinions of how you choose to manifest your creativity. You don't let whether or not you were paid to publish define how you feel about your book. Being indie also has many privileges not afforded to traditionally published authors. It means that you get to be flexible and nimble. You can try things out, and you can learn from your mistakes. You can think outside the box and experiment, because the indie mentality is about believing that the way things have always been done is not necessarily the only way that things should be done. I'm going to get into this a lot more in Chapter 7, "Subverting the System While Working Within It," but it's a fact that things get myopic inside organizations that have been around for a long time, doing "business as usual."

We see this trend in publishing in spades. People who've been in the industry for a long time worship at the altar of a system that functioned really well fifty years ago. They have blinders on about the ways in which the industry is changing, because they don't want things to change. Or, if they can see the extent to which things are changing, they long for things to go back to the way they used to be. There are innovative people in traditional publishing circles, yes, but the prevailing mentality is the same as it's always been: adhere to a model that involves spending a whole bunch of money to acquire books and then not seeing most of those investments through.

Do I think that indie authors can uproot the traditional paradigm? Yes. I think it starts with our banding together in force to say that we are proud, that we will not stand for being segregated or discriminated against. Together we have to insist upon the adoption of new measures for measuring a book's worth—and that it not be based on whether an author has paid for their own work to be published. We need more community-oriented endeavors, which are prevalent in other industries. In his article, Vinjamuri referenced Indiecade.com, a conference for game developers, and independent film festivals, like Sundance and Tribeca, that celebrate indie filmmakers. Publishing has nothing that even approximates these events, and indie authors need strength in numbers to legitimize ourselves and to have forums where we can discuss ending this era of black-and-white thinking about publishing.

For indie authors, the very act of choosing ourselves—of green-lighting our own work—means going against the grain and sometimes dealing with, and needing to confront, those voices that will insist that anything outside traditional publishing is a second-tier option. Green-lighting your own work will force you to confront critics of all stripes, who will accuse you of vanity publishing (wielding that term as a weapon), and bar you from reviews, contests, and associations. The bias against self-publishing also extends into bookstores, which often have policies against print-on-demand (a euphemism for self-published) books. When forced to defend your work or your choices, you will have to grow a thick skin. You will be pushed not only to confront your choices, but also to articulate them. The good news is that you are hardly alone; the growing indie movement has strength in numbers, in the form of many examples of successfully self-published authors to point to.

And don't be sheepish about having invested in yourself. As

indie authors, because we put our money where our mouth is, we have an emotional investment in our work that is different than that of traditionally published authors. Once you decide to invest in your work, something shifts. You are taking a risk on yourself because maybe no one else will. The buck stops with you, and you call the shots. You become the decision-maker, not only on questions about how you want your book to go out into the world in terms of its professionalism—design, editorial, endorsements, etc.—but also in terms of the efforts you'll put forth in the arena of marketing and publicity. I've known too many authors over the years who've gotten modest-to-large advances and chosen not to reinvest in themselves as authors. They think (again, operating again from a very old-school mentality) it's the publisher's responsibility to do so. And when the publisher doesn't deliver, they're disappointed, and the publisher finds on its hands a burdensome author who's not grateful and not holding up their end of the bargain, and so this cycle repeats itself over and over again.

Whether or not you've ever fantasized about being (or expected to be) paid to write, a certain freedom comes with making your peace with going indie and then discovering the community that's out there, joining the ranks, talking with others about publishing and books and ways to be even more awesome than you already are. Being out and proud about your creative work and how you did it, and having zero tolerance for being defined by whether you invested in your own work, is critical. We are apparently the holdouts among our indie brothers and sisters, the only industry not celebrated for the courage it takes to invest in our own work. We can and will change this. It takes showing up, doing our work, publishing well, and telling our stories. It's just a variation on the work we're already doing as writers.

Chapter 3.

The Five *P*'s of Publishing Success

O ver the course of my publishing career, I've worked with every kind of personality imaginable—from hyperfocused writers who lay down tomes of content every week to those who struggle to eke out a few hundred words over the same time period; from authors with multiple books under their belts to total newbies; from writers who self-publish a first book, catch the publishing bug, and become multibook authors (and publishers) to those who get their one book out and will never publish again. No matter the personality, the five *p*'s at the heart of this chapter—patience, perseverance, platform, publicity, and prolificness—are cornerstones of making it as an author.

But before we delve more deeply into the five *p*'s, I want to talk about aptitude, which also can't be discounted. I believe that in order to be successful, an author needs to learn about the book publishing industry. There are those who excitedly embrace the challenge, growing from hobbyists to author experts with each new book they write and publish, and there are those who simply don't have the energy or whose curiosity extends only so far. Not every author can become an expert in the business. There's a lot to learn, after all, and if this isn't your primary industry or source of income, it may be too demanding. However, there are some basics that every author needs to understand to be successful, and, as the following story illustrates, educating yourself can pay off in long-lasting ways.

Once upon a time (because this is how all good fairy tales start), a debut author with a new book out flew to Nashville because he got a bee in his bonnet about meeting his sales force. He got in a cab and showed up unannounced at his distributor's office space in La Vergne, Tennessee. This author had been published by a major press, so Ingram was a wholesale account for him, and he wanted to understand the inner workings of the wholesale business and how it would impact his book sales. He asked a lot of questions, took a lot of notes. Someone from the office then drove him from their campus back to Nashville. In the car on the way to the city, the nice rep who'd been tapped to drive the author to his hotel told him everything he knew, best practices, about the industry. They chatted for a good forty-five minutes, and the author bade his driver farewell with a hearty handshake and a thank-you. Months later, the author's book hit the best-seller list. The author was John Grisham, and his debut novel was *The Firm*. And, yes, John Grisham lived happily ever after.

This story, in addition to making me admire Grisham more than I already did, highlights an author who was serious about his publishing endeavor. His publisher did not send him to Tennessee to meet with Ingram. He did this on his own initiative. He wanted to understand the wholesale side of the business specifically, but he also asked a lot of questions and took heed. We can't know all the factors that have played into Grisham's success; certainly, his writing and compelling plots are part of it, but no author is successful based solely on the merits of their writing alone. On the one hand, it's true that it's not enough just to write a book, and on the other, it's true that you can't just build your brand and expect to have success. Success comes from all the moving parts working together, steadily and consistently, over a long period of time.

Patience

I've already told you there's no magic bullet. In the same vein, there's also no quick fix for authors trying to figure out how to make themselves more attractive to publishers. I work with authors who are desperate to get traditionally published. For them that's the gold standard, and they either don't have the desire to self-publish or don't have the aptitude to do what it takes to become an entrepreneurial author (and that's okay!). But these authors are the ones most likely to be swayed by the notion that they can hire someone to make their dreams come true. These are the authors who think someone like me can give them a referral to an agent who will say yes and sell their book to a publishing house—done deal. But it doesn't work like that.

In book publishing, whom you know matters only to a certain extent. Your connections can open doors, and having endorsements from well-known people can make you look more polished and desirable. But these things alone will not make you a successful author. In fact, the only way to achieve the kind of success you probably admire in the authors you most love is to put your head down and produce. Authors do not become famous, beloved household names overnight—first, because it (usually) takes more than one book to break out. Yes, some authors have success with a first book, but then, if no second book is forthcoming, they will fizzle out.

Consider Christina Baker Kline, author of *The Orphan Train*. Kline is not an overnight success story—she had eight previously published books to her credit before *The Orphan Train* became a best seller. And there are countless other stories just like this. Although we certainly hear about breakout debut authors, by and large the authors who pursue their craft and diligently toil away, climbing their way from obscurity to having some degree of name recognition, are the real success stories.

On the self-publishing side, patience sometimes entails knowing when to abandon your current course of action to try something new. Tracy E. Banghart, author of *Shattered Veil*, epitomizes a patient author trying to do everything right. She landed an agent easily, but then the agent couldn't sell the work. After a certain period of time, she moved forward with self-publishing. After receiving a starred *Publishers Weekly* review, she was interviewed by the magazine and asked why she decided to self-publish. She said, "I got to the point where I stopped being willing to let someone else determine my value as a writer."

The other place where patience comes into play is with your author platform (which we'll be discussing in this chapter). You need to build your author platform, but it cannot be built overnight; doing so is a marathon, not a sprint. Someone once tweeted me with this question: "Brooke, are you still working on your author platform?" My response: "Yes, and I will be forever!" Forever is a long time, but I wasn't exaggerating. With platform, there is no destination. It's an exercise in patience because it's an exercise in consistency. You must show up, create content, engage people, and generally work to feed the engine. If you look at writing and everything that's involved in maintaining a presence out in the world as a means to an end, you will exhaust yourself, and you might give up before you arrive. It's not a means to an end. It's a lifestyle. Which is why I am encouraging you to be patient. Keep at it. Keep writing. Keep publishing. Write whether or not anyone is listening.

Perseverance

You cannot and will not make it in this industry without this quality. I've never met a single published author for whom the entire experience—from the idea to having the book in hand—has been a linear or easy process. Everyone's journey is different. But you cannot write a whole and meaningful book without perseverance. You know that if you've completed a book. You breathe it if you've written more than one or if you have a daily writing practice.

It takes perseverance to write, but it also takes perseverance to follow through on everything else you must do both to get published and then to succeed. John Grisham showed incredible perseverance in taking a trip to Nashville to visit his wholesaler. This is the very essence of follow-through. He followed his desire to understand how his books got out into the marketplace through to an action, to meetings, to engaging book people who were happy to share their knowledge with him. Grisham would have heard from the Ingram folks a few tips about how to be a successful author: sign books at bookstores; get to know the bookstore events people; ingratiate yourself to people in the industry who make decisions; don't ever stop pitching your ideas; find ways to continue to make yourself and your content relevant.

In 2014, She Writes Press author Jill Smolowe published a memoir called *Four Funerals and a Wedding*. In it she shares her experience of loss—of losing her husband and three other loved ones all within seventeen months of one another. The memoir saw good sales for a grief memoir (something people in the industry forewarned would make it a hard sell). One year later, Sheryl Sandberg's husband died suddenly while on vacation in Mexico. Three days later, Smolowe published a piece on Fortune. com called "What Not to Say to Sheryl Sandberg." Smolowe is an expert on grief by virtue of lived experience, and also from having published her memoir. She's in a unique position to know exactly what people should not say to a grieving widow and has positioned herself as a go-to person on her topic. Yet the fact that this piece ran on Fortune.com a full year following the publication of *Four Funerals and a Wedding* showcases Smolowe's perseverance. She's keeping in mind that she has something to say on this topic, and when a high-profile person loses a spouse, she has something meaningful to contribute—something that's helpful to people beyond just Sandberg. Smolowe seized an opportunity to get her message out to a wider audience.

There will never be a shortage of these kinds of opportunities for authors, but you have to look for them and then act when things happen. First, you have to believe that you have something to say. Then you have to be able to act fast. You have to pitch yourself and be ready to churn out a piece quickly—sometimes the very same day news breaks. Authors can't just write their books and then sit back and wait. They have to find ways to leverage their book's existence by finding outlets where they can contribute content—blogs, magazines, newspapers. If you want to succeed, you have to keep your eyes open and your ear to the ground. And then you have to be poised to pitch, write, and deliver. Perseverance.

Platform

Platform is a topic I write about, teach about, and speak about—and therefore feel particularly passionate about. In my last book, I dedicated a whole chapter to this topic and called it "The Almighty Author Platform." I love to teach about platform because of the degree of misunderstanding that exists about what it is, and because there's so much resistance to it. These two things make it a rewarding subject—because I have the opportunity, on a regular basis, to steer people toward a better relationship with their author platform. And a better relationship with your budding or growing platform is another key component to succeeding as an author.

The following pie chart is something I created to counter a myth I see out in the world around author platform, which is that it's all about social media. My simple response to that is that it's not. In my pie chart, I give social media only 10 percent, and that's because it's an effective tool, most effective at measuring the fact that people follow you. But it's not effective at getting

What An Author Platform Is Made Of

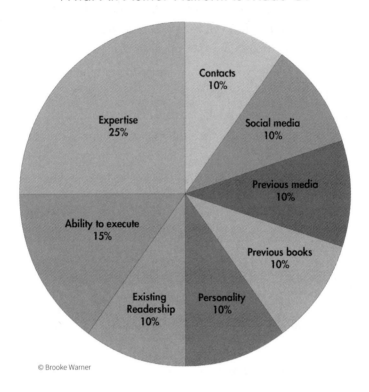

© Brooke Warner

people to do things, like buy books, and therefore it's only one piece of the author platform, and not the most important piece.

Platform is more than just a buzzword or an industry obsession. It's something you actually have to pay attention to if you want to sell books. It's about visibility and growing an audience for your work. Agents and editors are looking for authors with platforms because their platform suggests that they have a built-in readership. In 2011, my last year at Seal Press, I acquired a book called *Toss the Gloss*, by Andrea Robinson. Robinson had almost no social media presence, no other books, and not much by way of prior media. She couldn't showcase that she had a strong existing readership, either. What she had was a well-known agent from whom I had bought books in the past and whom I trusted when she told me Robinson would execute. Her contacts were stellar—including Ralph Lauren, who ultimately gave her a blurb and threw her a launch party. She was also clearly an expert on her topic, maybe even an industry leader, having worked in the beauty industry for decades. Seal made a strong offer for the rights to publish her book. I share this story because Robinson exemplifies the kind of author who's getting a book deal without social media, but it helps you, too, to understand the things publishers are looking at when they decide what books they want to acquire—and why.

Let's take a moment to break down each of the areas of this pie chart:

AUTHOR EXPERTISE (25 PERCENT)

Not all authors are blind to what their expertise is, but too many are. I get authors—especially novelists and memoirists—telling me all the time (whining, honestly). *But I'm not an expert in anything!* Nothing makes my hair stand on end more than a statement like this, but it also gets me fired up to help that person immediately to change their tune.

If you are writing a book, you need to get comfortable with the title of expert. It doesn't matter what kind of book you're writing. If you are writing a novel or a memoir, you are an expert on the issues you are writing about. If you've lived through something, whatever it is, you have experiential expertise, and if your manuscript focuses on something you know enough to have written a whole book about it, then you can translate that expertise into building a platform.

One exercise I find helpful is to ask yourself why you're the person to be writing your book. If you can't answer this question, please think about it. Consult with others. Really figure it out, so that by the time your book comes out you'll be able to talk effortlessly about what inspired you and what uniquely qualifies you to write this book. At the heart of the answer you ultimately come up with should be your unique experience—what you bring to the table that no one else but you could have brought. Let what you write in response to this question be free-flowing, and also acknowledge your strengths, talents, and knowledge as you work on it. Too many of us tend to undervalue our abilities; the first step toward being an expert is believing that you can be an expert. You may have to fake it till you make it, but this exercise in helping you define "why me?" will give you the motivation and validation you need to get there.

CONTACTS (10 PERCENT)

Everyone you know is a contact. The more people you know, the more influence you have, especially if you know people in high places. So what if those influencers are a couple degrees of separation from you? The ways in which some people choose to support fledgling authors are surprising. I've witnessed seriously established authors supporting new writers just because it feels good and because they remember what it was like to be in that position.

The other way you want to think about your contacts is in the context of your database. If you don't have a database, get one. Just set one up. Take that baby step. It takes a long time to build a meaningful list of contacts, but you cannot build one if you don't have a contact management system (CMS). When you're ready (and, I'm presuming, you have a website), you put a sign-up form on your home page. This is where writers again like to protest. "Who's going to want to sign up for my list? Do people really want to get more e-mail?"

Here's my response to these kinds of concerns. Imagine you have something you are trying to sell, but you don't have a storefront or a sign. When people finally manage to find you, you're not there, and you don't provide your phone number or any way for your eager customer to stay in touch with you. This is what you are effectively doing if you don't put a sign-up sheet on your website. You are denying people the opportunity to connect with you. You are choosing the idea that other people are too busy to want to receive messages from you. When people come to your website, the highest compliment they can pay you is to sign up for your site. They are saying that they want to hear more from you. These are your true fans—the people most likely to buy your book when you actually have something to promote. Don't get so caught up in self-defeating behavior (because that's what it is to suggest that people won't want to hear from you) that you sabotage real opportunities to build a fan base and to own people's contacts.

Contacts (in the form of names and e-mail addresses) are gold. When I do webinars, I often advertise on Facebook and Twitter, and the result of that outreach is negligible. I may get a handful of sign-ups (four or five people). If I e-mail the same message to my contact list of a few thousand people, the response is overwhelming: I often get as many as two or three hundred people on board. So take heed, and don't expect too much too soon. This effort is the same as everything else—a marathon. Take baby steps, and focus on building an engaged list of readers through regular contact and content they really want to read.

SOCIAL MEDIA (10 PERCENT)

I have written that social media does not a platform make, but that doesn't mean I think it's unimportant. Book publishers like social media because it gives us concrete numbers. We can see how many followers you have, and it's a baseline for your visibility and popularity. But social media is frustrating for new adapters and often leads to defeatism: when new authors start up on social media, they often give up too early because they're not getting enough followers fast enough. But, again, remember the marathon. After actively working on my Facebook fan page for nearly four years, I finally passed the two-thousand-likes mark. I felt like I earned every single one of those likes, even though there were many days where the effort didn't seem worth it. I know firsthand the uphill battle for the concrete numbers. Nevertheless, I recommend that all authors be on social media.

It's not so important what you do but that you do what you do consistently. There's been a lot of debate about whether to have a Facebook fan page or just a profile page. Honestly, it doesn't matter that much one way or another. What matters is that the people who are following you care about your message.

The reason I have a profile that I keep separate from my fan page is that my high school friends and family don't want to get my daily posts about publishing. But for some people, their platform is an extension of themselves and their personality, and so it doesn't matter—and friending people on Facebook and using that forum as a platform-builder works just fine.

If you don't like Facebook, don't be on it. But be on something. Maybe you like Twitter better. Great. Many novelists I work with use Pinterest. Anyone with a very visual book—lifestyle, cooking, photography, etc.—should consider Pinterest, since image sharing is the most popular and effective form of social media out there. If your work lends itself to video, do YouTube. Experiment to find a social media channel that works for you and your writing. In the beginning, keep it simple. Three to four posts a week is a good, steady place to start, and you can grow from there.

PREVIOUS MEDIA EXPERIENCE (10 PERCENT)

If you're starting at zero, you may not have any media experience, by which I mean TV, radio, podcasts, and video—media that requires you to be forward-facing and engage with your audience. There are easy ways to get this kind of experience, however, in a homegrown way. You can put videos of yourself up on YouTube or develop a fun series idea that would lend itself to video. I once worked with an author who'd written a memoir about growing up as an undertaker's daughter. She concocted a plan to videotape herself doing little dispatches from the graveyard, all about ways to honor the dead—including grave etchings, tending gravesites, and honoring the deceased through ritual. I thought this was a brilliant idea, and the author did, too, but she didn't follow through on it.

When I'm working with a coaching client, I don't take a hard stance on not following through on ideas. After all, sometimes we're just brainstorming. This author might not have had the gumption to figure out who would have done the taping. Maybe she felt silly. Maybe she didn't like the way she looked on video. I had this experience when I started videotaping myself during the writing of my last book. But an interesting thing happened after three or so videos: I got more comfortable, both on camera and with watching myself.

Since then, I've had myself taped a few times: speaking in front of an audience, interviewing memoirist Mary Karr (an exciting one!), and presenting on panels. I've put those all up on YouTube. This is nothing huge, but it showcases how simple "media experience" can be if you don't have a TED talk or if you've never been on TV before. Note that audio counts here as well. If you're not a video person but can envision yourself doing a talk you can record, you can do so simply by using a free conferencing tool like FreeConference.com. Figure out what you're going to talk about, and then record yourself and post the audio file online.

PREVIOUS BOOKS WRITTEN (10 PERCENT)

So, you're working on your first book. Totally fine. But how long have you been writing it, and how long do you think it'll be before you finish? If you think it's going to take another two or three years before you get your book published, consider self-publishing an e-book. It might remain an e-book forever, or you might decide later to turn it into a print book. I did this with my book, *Breaking Ground on Your Memoir*, coauthored with Linda Joy Myers. We put it out as an e-book in early 2015 and then started getting enough requests that we turned it into a print book later that year. This was a great way to spread out our expenses on the book, and having first published it digitally gave us some insight into whether we would have an audience for a print version.

With an e-book, you will have an Amazon presence. You will have a book credit to your name. You can call yourself an author. Not enough people acknowledge the value of written content as a platform-builder, though it's a simple enough concept. The more you write, the more you'll show up. The more consistently you publish—online, in e-book form, in book form—the more your readers will see that you are someone with good, interesting content and with something to say.

Media opportunities come to authors who have published work, and less so to writers who are working on a book. So get out there, and don't just create—produce! And then let people know you're producing. You have to balance providing value to your readers with self-promotion, but if you publish something and then don't talk about it, you're still on square one. You move toward your goal of becoming a successful author by first becoming a published author, and you have nothing to lose by self-publishing content on your way to figuring out what you'll do with your print book or books—and you'll learn a lot about publishing (and what you'll do better next time) along the way.

AUTHOR'S PERSONALITY (10 PERCENT)

I first read Jeff VanderMeer's *Booklife* in 2011, when I was writing my first book, which happened to coincide with my own decision-making about how I wanted to interact and engage online. VanderMeer helped me understand that authors get to choose who they want to be online. You can create a persona, and you don't have to bring every aspect of yourself online. In fact, you should actively strive *not* to be one of those people who overshare, posting about every little thing, when you're trying to position yourself as an expert on one particular thing.

There's real value to figuring out who you want to be online. And this doesn't mean that you are disingenuous; it means simply that you're choosing what matters to the readership you've decided you want to engage. I write about writing and publishing, and what I put on social media is therefore about writing and publishing. Once in a blue moon, I put up a post about my son, usually a photo. If I did this excessively, people would get tired of it; the reason they've liked my page is not to hear about what I'm up to every day with my family, but rather to gather information about writing and publishing.

Through this information, I also bring myself. I'm forthcoming and share about my life to a certain degree in my posts, but I also am not a memoir writer, like Anne Lamott, who shares tons and every day on her personal Facebook page because she's set a precedent for her readers—through being a memoirist and through this kind of self-exposure—and this is what they expect to see. Elizabeth Gilbert has a fantastic and popular Facebook feed, where she shares a lot about herself personally, albeit through a lens of self-expression and creativity, because this is part of the personality she brings to her work. It's authentically her, but it's focused and clear, and her posts are relevant and on point with the brand that is Liz Gilbert.

As important as it is to figure out who you want to be online, don't let figuring it out stop you from getting started. You might morph over time and refine your message as you receive feedback on various posts you write, figuring out who your audience is and what they respond to. Whatever you decide, know that having boundaries is okay and that wanting to be private is not an excuse for not being online. You can be a very private person and still have a successful strategy for putting your content out on your site and on your social media platforms.

Notice any judgments or reservations you might have about being visible online. I know all the messages: *Who's going to care? Other people are doing this better than I am. Why am I bothering with this? What's the point?* I have worked with writers who believe that the very act of putting themselves out there is boastful and self-aggrandizing. Plenty of writers think they don't know what to blog about or that they don't have enough to say. If you feel this way, it's because you have not figured out what your message is. You might start by brainstorming the five main themes of your book, especially if you're writing a memoir or a novel. I have countless clients who've been able to develop meaningful platforms from novels—writing about parenting; grief and loss; writing; fashion; relationships; and more.

Another reason people don't put themselves out there is that they're shy or they think they have to have everything figured out. Some writers are such perfectionists that executing a single post takes weeks, when it should take hours. Part of the fun of being online and growing your platform is engaging. Don't forget that. Building an audience is about letting people get to know you and having conversations. In the beginning, people may not comment on your posts. Don't worry. Comment on other people's posts. Be a good citizen in the online world. Compliment and share other people's work. Fully embrace your generosity. If you already have a firm handle on who you are and how you show up online, fabulous, but if you have reservations or know that you've been holding back, it's not too late. Get out there and interact—and be yourself and figure out your boundaries as you go along.

ABILITY TO COME THROUGH, OR
TO EXECUTE (15 PERCENT)

The ability to execute, like personality, is sort of a "soft" aspect of author platform, but it matters. It's about follow-through and the ability to stick to a commitment to create content. It's about consistency and showing up even if it seems like no one is listening. Building an author platform is grueling work, but it's truly rewarding when you see the occasional spikes in engagement or new followers, or payoff in the form of positive feedback or sales. I don't fault the client I mentioned above who didn't follow through on her video series—there are a million reasons and excuses not to do things that support your platform. The way you treat your platform will be indicative of the way you treat your future book campaign(s), however, so consider how serious you want to be with all of this. If you want to tread lightly, that's a legitimate approach, but don't be disappointed later if you're not getting the results you want. You might get a lucky break, but even lucky breaks are the result of hard work—like a blog post going viral. The successes of the authors I know who are in the trenches come from hard work and follow-through.

Just as you don't run a marathon without training for weeks or months, you don't start your author platform full-force. Building your platform takes discipline and hard work, but if it weren't worth it, no one would be doing it.

The key is to find genuine value in your endeavors. Keep going, even when you feel as if no one is listening. Eventually people will start to listen, and eventually you will get a comment on a post that makes you realize you're making a difference, reach a surprising milestone with your contacts, or connect with a high-profile writer who supports you just because.

Have faith. Work hard. Don't dismiss these ideas just because they feel like too much effort or because starting from zero seems daunting. Everyone started from zero, even your literary heroes. And it's only with hindsight and effort that anyone has the wisdom to promise that it's worth it.

I promise it is. Come on in and test the waters. Wade in slowly. You'll find your way.

Publicity

Let me start the publicity conversation with a simple and clear bit of advice: spend the money.

Most authors I work with suffer from an affliction called high expectations. I can't fault them, either, because I experienced it myself, as much as I was surprised when it snuck up on me. When I started writing my first book, I had modest expectations. This was a wonderful diagnosis because it meant that I wasn't placing too much pressure on myself. I wanted to publish a book that would establish me as an author-expert. I realized that if I wanted to have a thriving business, I needed to have a book. Also, as the cofounder and publisher of She Writes Press, which was brand new at the time, I decided to be the guinea pig and first author through the process and out of the gate, in 2012. I needed to see whether there were any unanticipated kinks. I'd also never written a book before and didn't expect it to be my last, so my thought when it came to publicity was that I would just do the minimum and then see what happened.

I hired a publicist and told her about my modest expectations. She created a publicity campaign that was aligned with my expectations and my budget, and all was well—until my book came out. In the early weeks of its being out in the world, I was shocked by how much I wanted people to know about it. I'd somehow thought, because I was in book publishing and had experienced the publication of so many books over the years, that I was going to be a super-easygoing author, cool with the modest expectations I'd laid out for myself. I decided on what back then I called a "viral approach" to publicity. To my mind, that meant my book would get whatever attention it was going to get just from my blogging about it and having a press release and allowing the publicist I hired to do some limited pitching. Needless to say, nothing went viral. I got a few hits, and that was it.

When I freaked out about how little was happening with my book, my publicist gently reminded me of my modest expectations. She asked me, kindly, if anything had changed. I had to give this some serious thought. Did I want to ratchet up my campaign or sit with the plan and the budget we'd laid out? In the end, we stuck with the original plan. It was a good lesson for me because it helped me to experience what it meant to want to be acknowledged for my work. It's also helped me in the years since to explain to authors the real value of publicity, which is significant, especially if you have high expectations.

You might start interviewing publicists and decide that it's prohibitively expensive. Many authors I work with are simultaneously financing their own production and print run, so a publicity campaign can feel like a hard expense to swallow. And yet without it, your book will not move. There is simply too much competition in today's publishing climate to believe that your book can or will go anywhere based on the merits of your writing alone. I used to believe in a ripple effect—that you could "let it ride" and see what happens. But I no longer believe this, because I've seen the ripple effect prove ineffective. There is nothing more important to a book's success than a well-orchestrated publicity campaign that you initiate at least six months in advance of your book's release date.

Five Things to Do When You're Hiring a Publicist

This article comes from Crystal Patriarche, CEO of SparkPoint Studio, parent company of She Writes Press since 2014.

Hiring a publicity person or firm can be scary. It's expensive, there's no guarantee of results, and the situation often feels elusive and out of your control—as if there's some magic formula or secret and you are not in on it.

To give your book its most promising shot, you should look for publicists with a good mix of experience, personality, price, energy, intelligence, confidence, ambition, relevance (to you and to the market), and results.

Here are five things you can do to make the process less scary and cumbersome, as well as more likely to succeed:

1. Research. You wouldn't buy a car without doing some due diligence, right? You would probably ask your friends or post on social media to solicit opinions on what vehicles are best, given your goals and needs. You'd probably also do research online to find out what features and models are available and to read reviews.

So before you hire a publicist, you must do some research and solicit the advice of publishers and writers who have hired publicists before. Check out authors you love and whose platforms you admire, and see who they work with. Ask authors who write in your genre or on your subject. Ask agents, editors, author friends, and support groups.

Also, find out which publicists authors worked with early in their careers. A lot of times, authors move up to larger or more expensive firms for their PR, but it was those "little people" who helped them get there and made it easier for the bigger firms that picked them up when they were finally established.

When you see books covered in the media, online, or in print, see if you can find out whether a publicist was involved and, if so, who that publicist was.

Then create a list of candidates your research has identified and try to schedule phone interviews or meetings with each firm or freelancer. Be sure you have a number of options (you may be surprised by how many times you won't get any response). And create talking points for each publicist on your list (who referred you; what you liked about this person or firm, based on their website; what concerns you have, based on what you've read and/or heard; and so on).

2. Prepare a list of questions. Before those phone interviews or meetings—and in addition to your notes for each one—prepare a list of questions you want to cover during the conversation. Don't let publicists derail you by dropping names and mentioning media outlets they guarantee. While that sort of information can be nice to know, especially if the guaranteed media outlets are good ones, you should be sure you also cover the things you want to learn—things like:

- How long have you been doing book publicity?
- How do you select clients?

(continued on next page)

- Do you read your clients' books?
- Have you read my book?
- Who will be my main contact?
- What can I expect in terms of communication and reporting?
- What can I expect in terms of results? (Knowing that no one can guarantee results, you should look for someone who is realistic and practical when responding but who also seems confident and nimble.)
- Who are your current clients?
- How many clients do you have at any one time?
- How big is your team?
- What is your biggest success?
- What's your biggest challenge?
- Why should I hire you?
- Why do you want to work with me?
- What differentiates you from other publicists?
- What is the expected timeline and process?
- How do you resolve conflict?
- How often will I hear from you?

3. Ask for references. Don't hire someone based on one great conversation; they might have wooed you with words you wanted to hear. Be sure to ask each publicist for references—a list of current clients and past clients. The list can work as a red flag if it doesn't include anyone the publicist worked with recently or if the publicist seems to have too many clients all at once.

4. Interview those references. Don't just ask for the references; follow through. E-mail and call and have a list of questions for those references as well—things like:

- What did you hire this publicist to do?
- What was the experience like?
- Were you happy with the experience?
- How was the communication?
- Was there anything you wanted done differently?
- What was the biggest success?
- What was the biggest challenge?
- What was the publicist's work style?
- What are this publicist's strengths and weaknesses?

And don't stop with the references a publicist gives you. Get on the publicist's website, find a few other clients, and interview them, too.

If clients had negative experiences with a publicist, you don't have to rule out the publicist or assume that they're hiding something. Talk with the publicist again, and bring up your concerns. Every campaign is different, and every client is different. Experiences that a client finds negative may relate to a very small budget or to unrealistic expectations or to things beyond the publicist's control.

Be sure to explore and think about both the good and the bad feedback until you feel confident and comfortable that you know what you need to know.

(continued on next page)

5. Listen to your gut. At some point, you are just going to click with someone. The energy is going to feel right; the things that person understands and communicates are going to resonate with you. You will know when this happens.

It may or may not happen with the publicist who has the biggest-name clients or the happiest clients; it may or may not happen with a publicist others are pushing you toward. Only you can know, and a gut check is a pretty good indicator.

If the passion and vibe didn't please you and you didn't feel confident or cared for during your communications, you'll probably have the same reactions during the publicity campaign. So listen to your gut, in addition to what those clients and authors said.

Prolificness

This final *p* is one that can feel the most laborious to authors, especially if they've just finished a new book and their publicist is demanding new content, and when, after three or six months, the advice you start getting if you want to stay on people's radar is to write a new book. *Write a new book? Didn't I just finish the last one?* I started thinking about writing this book about a year after the release of my first book, but it took me a full three years to get my ideas and energy together to write it. For some people, publishing a book a year is in their genetic makeup. It's part of a gift they have for being prolific. Writing and publishing a book three years after my first one feels pretty darn prolific to me. But in today's publishing climate, three to four years is probably the outside parameter of how long you should wait before publishing a next book if you want to be a successful author.

Most authors say that they start to notice a shift in overall sales once they publish their third book. The best articulation of why it takes a few books to start to move the needle on sales comes from Dean Wesley Smith, who likens an author's inventory to magic pies. It's really worth reading Smith's entire theory on magic pies in his own words, because it's convincing and fascinating and will motivate you to want to write more and more and publish more and more. The gist of Smith's magic-bakery metaphor is that your magic bakery is full of magic pies that reform every time you cut a slice. Each piece of the pie is a cash stream, and authors can earn serious money if they learn how to divvy up these pies, which involves learning a thing or two about copyright—the secret ingredient in these magic pies. Smith's point is twofold: 1) you can make a lot of money on a single book if you know where to look to sell off the pieces, and 2) you have to keep producing to keep your inventory high. Those shelves have to keep filling up with new pies. To read more about this whole intriguing idea, look for Smith's "Killing the Sacred Cows of Publishing: You Can't Make Money Writing Fiction."

Smith's whole theory hinges on prolificness, and becoming prolific is both a state of mind and a discipline. You become prolific once you decide that you have more than one book in you, and when you find ways to prioritize your writing as more than a hobby. In order to be prolific, you have to own the title of writer, and then you have to go out and claim the title of author.

Prolificness has nothing to do with how you choose to publish, either. It's for traditionally and indie published authors alike. In fact, the most prolific authors are the "hybrid authors," those who are publishing some books traditionally and some on their own. This journey toward publishing is about anything but being passive. Just as being prolific involves a clear choice to prioritize your writing, being a prolifically published author might mean that you will explore alternative and multiple publishing paths—including traditional; including nontraditional; including digital only; including writing articles and guest posting and posting on your own blog.

The nature of being prolific also means that you believe and embrace that you have a lot to say about your topic. It means that you will wear the title of thought leader and that you're contributing new ideas and information to your areas of expertise. It might also mean thinking about ways to "cross over," by which I mean leveraging one area of expertise into another. I'll reference Elizabeth Gilbert again here because she's done this so beautifully. She is a memoirist and a novelist, but she's also been able to convert her expertise into a platform that's about living a big and creative life, which she's parlayed into her book *Big Magic*. She followed the threads of her own passions to create this platform for herself, and if she ever doubted whether she had enough to say about creativity, you'd never know it.

Being prolific does not mean that you become pigeonholed. It doesn't mean that you regurgitate content or slog through the writing of a second book because you "have to." If you come up against an edge of doubt, wondering whether you can actually write a second book or fretting because you don't know what your next book is going to be about, hire someone to support your creative outlets. There are book coaches and creative types galore who can help you develop a book from the point of concept. There are countless workshops, classes, and forums that support the struggling creative genius in all of us when it's feeling locked up or buried underground. Don't let yourself get stuck in a pattern of thinking about writing all the time. That's its own kind of prison. It takes a regimented approach to your writing to make it a practice, and you might need some support at various times, but this last p is a big one for any writer with dreams of real success as an author. Go forth and do huge and amazing things in your writing life. Wow people. Embrace your dreams and soar to new heights. It's not going to be a clear, linear, or always fun and easy path, but if this is what you want, you will create a life that supports your writing.

Chapter 4.

How to Be Successful in Your Genre

Before you can be successful in your genre, you have to understand the role genre plays in the industry and how it drives a successful marketing and publicity plan, which in turn drives sales. Knowing about the genre you're writing in—fiction, memoir, romance, self-help, etc.—starts with reading in your genre. Though it's not a prerequisite that you be fully educated about the genre you're entering, reading the best-selling authors who've come before you and brushing up on the craft specific to your genre will give you a leg up. I'm astounded by the number of authors who come to me for coaching who admit that they don't read the genre they're writing in. Sometimes, especially with memoir writers, they even express disdain for their chosen genre. This stems from judgments people tend to heap onto memoir writing in general, that it's self-indulgent and, as Mary Karr calls it, a "ghetto-ass genre." (I'll get into this a bit more below.)

Tread carefully here. To be a successful author, you must be an ambassador to other writers aspiring to do what you will ultimately achieve. So pay attention along the way to who inspires you and why, and if you do harbor disdain for your genre, see what you might be able to do to change that. Gather up your inspirations like precious gemstones, and treat them with due regard. Your success in your genre, after all, starts with a foundation of an assumed readership for your book and with your belief that what you're writing will move, help, entertain, or intrigue certain people.

Because I teach both online and offline, I encounter what I call the "dissenter" almost every time I teach a class, hold a webinar, or sit on a panel. The dissenter is the person who believes that nothing I say applies to them because they're working in an outside genre, whatever they deem that genre to be. Sometimes that outside genre, per the dissenter's perception, is something as broad as all fiction. Other times, more reasonably, it's a legitimately specialized genre, like sci-fi/romance, or children's. The dissenter is generally well intentioned. They come to webinars or conferences wanting to gain information. They believe in their book just as much as the next writer. And oftentimes they're justified in their dissent because there is so much variation among the genres when it comes to marketing and selling successfully, and what works for a self-help author will not necessarily work for a novelist. It's not a problem, per se, to be a dissenter, because many of them know a lot; the problem is in defaulting to this position and not being willing to open yourself to possibilities because you've already made up your mind that certain courses of action or efforts aren't going to work for you.

Sometimes dissenters are superspecific and work to call out ways in which their genre differs from industry standards. For example, in 2015 I wrote a blog post called "3 Reasons to Keep Your Word Count Shorter Than 80,000 words." A writer of science fiction commented on the post that sci-fi and fantasy books are often longer, commonly one hundred thousand words, because it takes longer to world-build and because there's precedent for longer books in this genre in the marketplace. This was a great example of someone understanding their genre and what works in it and not being swayed by a generalization that was not necessarily true for what they were doing. To my earlier point, the more knowledge you obtain early on in your writing process about your genre, the better your chances of success— on all fronts. Even something like word count, for instance, has an impact on whether your book will find its way.

When it comes to doing the actual writing of our books, we're all in the same boat, no matter our chosen genre. No one escapes the fact that writing requires discipline. At the 2015 Bay Area Book Festival, while I was in the midst of struggling with my own discipline in writing this book, I attended a panel where Scott James, on behalf of his writing community, the Co-op, spoke of a formula for success he called the AC Ratio, the Ass-in-Chair Ratio, and its direct correlation to getting a lot of writing done. The idea is that the more often your butt is in the chair, the more writing you will get done. This amusing little formula was helpful to me as I considered what I needed to do to finish my book: get my butt in the chair more regularly, the same as any writer who wants their book to see the light of day. But beyond the process of writing your book, and hopefully well before you're done with your first draft, you will have delved deeply into what it means to be writing in the genre you're writing in. In this chapter, we're going to explore the following genres:

- Fiction, commercial and literary
- Memoir, commercial and literary
- Nonfiction, commercial and noncommercial
- Genre fiction (science fiction; fantasy; romance; urban fiction; erotica; and any other fiction subgenre that I might not address)
- Self-help/how-to
- Young adult/middle grade/new adult
- Children's/picture book
- Outliers

The genre you're writing in is like a club you're joining. You want to know the other members in that club, to learn from them at first, and maybe eventually to teach and mentor them. There are outside parties that cater to your club of choice, and you want to pay attention, when the time comes, to working with people who know something about your club and its rules, values, and tested ways of doing things. You will eventually be building relationships with these outside parties to create a team to support you. These people may include an editor, an agent, a publisher, a book designer, a publicist, and anyone else on your team, from social media experts to marketing specialists to e-book strategists. And while your team is hugely important to your success, once you have that all in place, don't forget about your club. This is your community, your people. Be a connector and an advocate. Part of being successful in your genre means absorbing everything there is to know about your genre, knowing the people who are writing in your genre, and engaging in the broader conversation—online and offline—about issues of importance to writers and readers in your genre.

What's the Difference Between Genre and Category?

We know that genre is a category of literary composition, but why does it matter? A post called "Genre Descriptions (Fiction Only)," on AgentQuery.com, articulates a great response to "why genre matters" with the simple statement that genres are "a staple of the publishing world." Genre is a classification system, subject to change over time and based on trends. For instance, right now we're witnessing the rise of a new genre called new adult, a fiction genre that's different from young adult (YA) because it skews a little older (ages eighteen to twenty-four), whereas YA has typically been targeted at people ages twelve to eighteen. This came about because authors and publishers saw a market for new adult (older readers reading YA) and believed that YA wasn't representing what they were doing, and so they needed a new genre. And that's how it happens.

Now let's turn to category, which for book publishing purposes is a division within a system of classification, which is sliced and diced hundreds of different ways. At a very high level, you have two categories: fiction and nonfiction. These are like the X and Y chromosomes of all written material. It's pretty much either/or, with a handful of experimental authors throwing a wrench into this binary (just like actual biology). Within these two big categories, you find your identity, your self-expression. This is your genre, and there are a lot of genres to choose from. Some people have genre identity crises that create confusion, just like in the real world. A writer might call their book a "fictionalized memoir," for instance, because they're straddling the line between memoir and fiction. Another writer may have written women's fiction, but the book is also a thriller and has hints of romance. These writers are tempted to explain the ways in which their books defy or cross genres, but they shouldn't. Publishing, after all, is not particularly progressive when it comes to futzing with its classification systems, and you're not a rebel because you're trying to be clever or span three genres; you're just an amateur.

After you choose one (yes, just one) genre, you'll come back to category. To continue our analogy, this next level of category is composed of your identifiers, the things that tag you as part of a group—like race, ethnicity, sexual orientation, where you grew up, your level of education, etc. If you think about these kinds of identifiers as the ways you connect in the world with other like-minded people, you'll understand how book categories are similar. You're looking to tag your book with identifiers (categories) that will draw interested readers. There's an old saying in book publishing that writers should not try to be all things to all people, and for good reason. You cannot appeal to everyone, and you don't want to. Identifying your book specifically, drilling down to the essence of what it is and naming it, is actually going to increase your chances of being read—because you're articulating for your readers what your book is, what it aims to do, and exactly whom it's for.

Categories are important to searchability on search engines like Amazon, notably, and other online retailers as well. Some marketing experts out there offer strategy services designed to get your book to number one in its category. You start this process by trying to drill down and figure out just how niche you can get while still being relevant. At the end of the day, the fact that people pay good money for these services proves my earlier point—that you can't and don't want to be all things to all people. Choose one genre, and then let your categories do the job they're supposed to do. You get to choose two to three, depending on your platform, and then usually up to seven keywords. Each piece of data you provide helps to paint a composite picture of your book, so spend time thinking through what you have and how you want to present your book to the world. Genre, category, and keywords alike impact how you talk about your book and your readers' ability to find it, so you want to read up on the differences and either choose well, if you're self-publishing, or collaborate with your publisher if you're able to.

A Brief Exploration of the Genres

Fiction, Commercial and Literary

We'll start with fiction because it's by far the most competitive of the genres. We're looking at commercial versus literary because these are the two primary categories of fiction the industry recognizes. There are subsets of fiction, too, including genre fiction, which we'll cover below, but a lot of other fiction subgenres—

like chick lit and women's fiction and upmarket fiction—are just spin-off terms that commercial or literary fiction encompass.

Commercial fiction, simply stated, is fiction that's high-concept (meaning easy to explain). It's the kind of fiction that makes summer reading lists. Commercial fiction includes chick lit, a lot of women's fiction, and most books that hit the best-seller list. Examples of commercial fiction are books like Maria Semple's *Where'd You Go, Bernadette*; Gillian Flynn's *Gone Girl*; and Nicholas Sparks's *See Me* (as well as everything else Sparks has ever written).

Literary fiction is basically a novel that's extremely well written. The language is elevated. It's not a beach read. It's the kind of novel you have to read slowly to make sure you're capturing the richness of the language. When you think of the masterpieces of fiction you've read, they're usually literary novels.

"Literary" often alludes to the notion that a piece of writing has achieved an elevated status, something beyond just "good writing." So it's a compliment to a writer to be called literary, yet literary work is notoriously difficult to sell. Sadly, I suppose, it's a commentary on our culture that publishers don't believe that there's enough of a readership to put out very many literary works, so they're loath to take risks on these kind of books, though of course they still do—occasionally. And so oftentimes the most talented authors are left with rejections full of high praise and wondering where they're going to go next. Literary novels include Donna Tartt's *The Goldfinch*, Anthony Doerr's *All the Light We Cannot See,* and Toni Morrison's *God Help the Child* (as well as everything else Morrison has ever written).

Memoir, Commercial and Literary

As with fiction, a commercial memoir is one that's high-concept, that a person can wrap their mind around instantly. Consider Elizabeth Gilbert's *Eat, Pray, Love*, a memoir that's as formulaic as it gets. Her concept is in her title: eating in Italy, praying in India, and loving in Indonesia. And the names of all the countries she visited start with an *I*. This was a highly commercial and highly acclaimed memoir, and its easy summarization is part of what defines it as commercial. Other examples of commercial memoirs include Cheryl Strayed's *Wild*, Issa Rae's *The Misadventures of an Awkward Black Girl*, and Sarah Hepola's *Blackout*.

Literary memoirs are just like literary novels—they're often gorgeously but densely written. They don't have that easy-to-pin-down description, even if they're highly thematic. *Angela's Ashes*, by Frank McCourt, is a literary memoir; so are all three of Mary Karr's memoirs—*The Liars' Club*, *Cherry*, and *Lit*—and Helen Macdonald's literary masterpiece, *H Is for Hawk*. What makes these memoirs literary is the level of the writing. The phrasing and craft are sophisticated. The authors may experiment with tense, sentence structure, and style. Just as with fiction, literary memoirists experience a lot of rejection, often from apologetic editors who love the work but can't acquire it.

Nonfiction, Commercial and Noncommercial

People often ask me how memoir is different from nonfiction, and my response is this: all memoir is nonfiction, but not all nonfiction is memoir. So I'm distinguishing nonfiction here as its own category, separate from memoir, but this is not to suggest that memoir is not nonfiction, because it is; it's just such a big genre, with its own specific rules, that it merits exploration on its own.

Here, I'll call out two strains of nonfiction: commercial and noncommercial. This is because nonfiction is one of the few genres where specifically noncommercial books are desirable to readers, and therefore to the publishing industry.

Just as in the prior genres, commercial is what it is—it's something writers can grab hold of. Well-known commercial nonfiction writers include Malcolm Gladwell, Barbara Ehren-reich, Jon Krakauer, and Mary Roach. These are authors who've executed multiple nonfiction books on topics that transcend a given niche. Commercial nonfiction often makes best-seller lists, because, it seems, the whole country is reading the book, or at least knows about it. Sometimes a book that's not partic-ularly commercial, like Naomi Klein's *This Changes Everything*, rises above the fray because it's so important and because even though it's hyperniche and might have been less commercial at another point in history, it's published at the right time, hit-ting a particular nerve and coinciding with a specific zeitgeist, movement, or cause.

Noncommercial nonfiction books are generally published by university presses or small, mission-driven presses. These are books that are important in some particular way even though their audience is known to be small. Sometimes they're art books or cookbooks that are geared toward readers at a particular level of expertise, so they're priced in such a way as to make them noncommercial. *Modernist Cuisine: The Art and Science of Cooking* (The Cooking Lab, 2012), a five-volume hardcover set, is priced at a cool $625, for example. But these kinds of books find their way because there's a readership willing to pay that kind of money to have them. *Modernist Cuisine* is an example of true artisan publishing, too, and many independently published authors are doing this kind of book on their own because they can't find a partner in the industry willing to support their projects financially.

Genre Fiction

Genre fiction includes but is not limited to science fiction, fantasy, romance, urban fiction, crime, thriller, horror, and erotica. The reason genre fiction exists separate from fiction is again because the rules for genre fiction are so different from commercial and literary fiction. The only thing tying together genre fiction and any other type of fiction, in fact, is that all forms are generated from the author's imagination. But other than that, genre fiction is a curious animal indeed, and each subgenre is truly its own culture.

Here more so than any genre we've touched on so far, writers will benefit tremendously from immersing themselves fully and wholeheartedly in the writer communities that support these genres. Unfortunately, as I write about more extensively in Chapter 1, some of the associations that exist to support writers explicitly ban self-published authors from their ranks. It's a shame, too, because genre fiction is proving itself to be the genre in which self-published authors are breaking the mold en masse. Hugh Howey is the poster child of sci-fi success, having sold his print rights to his book, *Wool*, to Simon & Schuster for a six-figure advance. Other popular genre fiction writers include Barry Eisler, who's written countless political thrillers; Amanda Hocking, who writes young adult urban fantasy and paranormal romance; and Stephanie Meyer of *Twilight* Fame.

Self-Help/How-To

Also a nonfiction genre, this differs from memoir and other nonfiction in its specific, prescriptive orientation. The dictionary definition of prescriptive is "giving exact rules, directions, or instructions about how you should do something," which is precisely what self-help and how-to aims to do. Many prescriptive books have list titles, like *Seven Habits of Highly Effective People* and *How to Talk So Kids Will Listen.* There is such a thing as a prescriptive memoir, but a book like that would still be a memoir if the story drives the book. If the story parts are supplemental, as is often the case in self-help books, where the author is using personal examples to illustrate a point, the book should be categorized as self-help.

There are many variations of the self-help book—from spiritual to business/leadership to crafting to writing. In this popular genre of book, experts share advice and knowledge with their readership, both for the purpose of educating, but also building their own expertise. Today, given the popularity of self-publishing, self-help and how-to books are exploding onto the marketplace. Most of the indie authors entering this genre are authors who have businesses and who want to publish a book as a calling card, or to attract more business.

I once heard a sales expert describe two types of businesses—vitamin and pills. She said you want to be the pill, because people need the pill, whereas the vitamin is just supplemental, and good for you. Self-help and how-to books are the pills of books, whereas fiction and memoir are the vitamins. This makes self-help easier to market and sell, as the built-in readership for these books are ostensibly people who need books on specific topics and are actively looking to buy them.

Middle Grade/Young Adult/New Adult

These genres are all about the age of the readership. Middle Grade (MG) is for readers 8 to 12; young adult (YA) for readers 13-17; and new adult (NE) for readers 18 to 24. This is one of the fastest-growing markets, due to the success of series like *Twilight, Divergent, Ender's Game,* and *Hunger Games.* As is the case with genre fiction, MG/YA/NE writers will do themselves a huge favor by getting cozy with their fellow writers in this genre, and researching the genre they're entering into. Content and voice are critical in this genre, and the wrong storyline or language can land you with a finished book that's not really appropriate for the target readership you think you're writing for. I've seen writers veer outside of what's deemed "appropriate" on both sides of the continuum, writing unsophisticated YA that felt like it would have been much more appropriate for a sixth-grader; and writing far too sophisticated YA, with sexual content and cuss words that seemed a bit too advanced for a thirteen-year-old, even if a seventeen-year-old might seek out a book like this.

A good editor can and will help you determine whether your book is appropriate for its audience. There are rules for these genres that will determine whether or not you have readers, let alone what kind of publishing path you end up pursuing. Like any genre, not knowing the rules of the genre will get you a swift rejection based on your query alone. For writers not intending to go the traditional route, these rules are equally important because they speak to the readership. For instance, MG books are less self-reflective in nature, because of the level of sophistication of the readers. The protagonists need to be a little older, because young readers want to read about kids who are older than they are. So if you have an idea for a MG/YA/NE book, read about the genres, and then read in your genre. If you're entering this genre blind, read at least ten books in your specific age range before you even get started. I'd recommend this for all genres, actually, but what's at stake here is greater because you might end up with a book that turns out not to be a fit for your intended audience.

Children's/Picture Book

This is one of the most difficult genres to break into, which is ironic in some ways because people often have a perception that writing a children's book is easy. It's not. A children's book, after all, is as much about the story as it is about the artwork. Children's books are also expensive to produce, both because of the layout and the four-color printing. Though every genre has its share of self-published success stories, you seldom hear about them where children's books are concerned because the best ones really do rise to the top. They're easier to judge and be judged because they're short, fast reads, and because readers determine quickly whether the art passes muster or not. Parents are the real judges of picture books, too, choosing books that might have a moral, or teach their kids a value.

This is an area of publishing that's contracting, even more so than other areas of publishing, though there will always be pockets of growth and adult trade publishers deciding they want to take a risk on a children's book. For instance, at Book Expo in 2015, Sounds True, a publisher that doesn't typically do children's books, was promoting its new release, *Good Night Yoga*, by Mariam Gates and Sarah Jane Hinder. The reason a publisher like Sounds True would take a risk on a book like this is that it saw both sales potential and an alignment of mission and values in the project. I was happy to see this book being published by Sounds True because it's a reminder that traditional publishers, especially small publishers, are taking risks and experimenting and publishing books that are on mission, regardless of their genre.

If you want to succeed as a children's book author, work with someone who can advise you. As I said, the art matters. Be careful not to get your ego wrapped up too tightly here if you're both the writer and the illustrator—or if your son is your illustrator. (I've seen this happen more than once.) Be open to feedback that you may need to partner with a different illustrator, and that you may need to pay that person handsomely for their work. There are children's-specific coaches and editors out there who specialize in this genre. Hire those people. Sure, it's possible that an expert will give you feedback that doesn't resonate, but if you get that same feedback twice or three times, listen, absorb, and then try to revisit your project with fresh eyes.

Outliers

A book is an outlier if it doesn't fit the industry's understanding of how a book should be categorized. Outliers include humor books (which are sometimes memoir or other nonfiction); books of essays (also sometimes memoir or other nonfiction); poetry; books of photography and some coffee table books; and adult coloring books (the newest rage).

Authors of outliers are in a tricky situation because the very nature of being an outlier means your book will be more difficult to sell. That might be because it's a genre like poetry, which few publishers want to take a risk on, or because you're trying to defy being categorized. It's important to understand, if you're in the former group, that belonging to a genre is a good thing. Agents and editors, as well as readers, want to put you into a mental category. Readers are looking for a certain type of book, based on what they like to read, and so if your book resists being "typed," it's less likely to be discovered.

Some authors may not realize that they have an outlier until they start to think about publishing options for their book. If you have a book that no one knows what to do with, it might be because it's an outlier, or it might be because it's trying to straddle two genres. For instance, a "fictionalized memoir" is not an outlier. It's just a novel. You may find that a simple tweaking of your language, or a willingness to conform, can make the difference here. If you're a true outlier, take heart. There are readers for poetry and essays, but you'll do yourself a favor early on if you temper your sales expectations.

There's No Right or Wrong Way

The reason I include a conversation about the genres in this book about green-lighting your work is that your genre typically impacts how you feel about your chances of getting traditionally published. Writers who enter into commercial nonfiction or memoir, for instance, usually do so because someone famous and successful has inspired them or because their friends and family have told them that they "must write a book!" Because this feeds into expectation and ego, getting to the point where you're going to finance your own book may be a long, hard road paved by letdown.

By contrast, many self-help authors are anxious to get their books out into the world by any means. They're entrepreneurs, and validation from the publishing world is less meaningful than publishing their work on their own timetable and under their own creative supervision. Then you have the genre fiction writers, who are blowing up self-publishing in a big way, publishing like gangbusters, making good money at it, and getting traditional deals left and right after their self-publishing success. Some are forging new ground as hybrid authors, publishing traditionally *and* self-publishing, depending on what they can negotiate and whether they want to retain certain creative control.

If you follow publishing, you'll see that it involves trends, just like any other industry. The trend in traditional publishing for the past decade has been toward the "sure bet" (i.e., the celebrity author). Sure-bet acquiring is maddening for editors. It puts them in a position of promoting traditional publishing's downward spiral and being unable to take risks on projects because of what's mandated from above. Conversations I've had with agents in the years since She Writes Press started have centered largely on the beautiful rejection letters they get from big-house editors. While these letters are surely sincere, I think they're also guilt-driven. When an editor spends a lot of time crafting a heartfelt response about why they can't acquire a book, it means they wish they could. Acquiring editors today get more accolades for their ability to get their hands on an author with a brand than they do on their ability to assess whether a manuscript really shines.

If you consider the contraction of traditional publishing, you might glean some insight into why genre fiction writers are doing so well in the world of self-publishing. One clear reason is that they've been barred from traditional publishing options for a longer period of time than other writers have. What novelists and memoirists are just now beginning to experience—too-high barriers to entry—genre fiction writers have been facing for years. They've been saying "oh well" to traditional publishing in response, and therefore they're leading the way. In addition, genre fiction writers are ridiculously prolific, and there seems to be a consensus that the writing within certain genres doesn't necessarily have to be executed flawlessly or even be particularly well edited for a book to see success (which differs greatly from literary fiction, where a few typos can result in mutiny from readers). The audience for these books is also a relatively known quantity. There's a big appetite for sci-fi/fantasy and romance and mysteries, and it's growing. And these readers read *a lot*.

Depending on what genre you're writing in, certain publishing options may look more attractive than others. In order to have a good shot at getting your book into libraries (important for most novelists), you need to be reviewed by *Library Journal* or *Booklist*. In order to rise above the noise, you need to get real publicity hits. My own experience of launching She Writes Press without traditional distribution was a huge wake-up call about the power of distribution, regardless of *how* you publish. This is another consideration for authors looking to make a splash with their books, one we'll cover in greater detail in Chapter 7. There is nothing straightforward about getting published if you want to do it right. Along the way, you will have pros and cons to weigh and tough decisions to make. But, as I said in Chapter 2 about the Indie Revolution, we are in the midst of uncertainty—which is a place where the proactive and flexible thrive, where nothing is static, and where what feels stable today could be upended tomorrow. Don't put all your eggs in one basket. Pursue all your options, and see if you can start to suss out what you like about various options and what you don't like about others. The better informed you are about what you're heading into, the more likely you are to have a good experience and to pave your own way for a strong future as a published author.

Chapter 5.

Your Book: Baby or Product?

Aspiring authors need, and often crave, information about publishing and how it all works so they can put their best foot forward. This book aims to dig beneath what's happening in publishing to give you just that. But authors also need support in giving shape to how they think about their books, how they position their books, and how they can live in the world as writers. In this chapter, we are going to examine your author mindset by stepping back for a moment to consider your relationship with your book and how your thinking about your book, while you're writing it and after it's published, impacts your success in ways you might not have imagined.

One of the reasons it can be hard for authors to greenlight their own books is that we often treat our books like our babies: they're an extension of us that we hope others will love and see as special. Authors relate to their books this way to such a degree that the baby metaphor is everywhere. They talk about being pregnant with an idea, incubating their work, giving birth to a book, laboring with their writing process. Most people are in fact pregnant with their book process longer than nine months, and the analogy stops working so fluidly when it comes to unconditional love. The inner critic rears its ugly head far too often for most authors to feel unabashedly in love with their books. Most authors go through a cycle, in fact.

I ran across the following tidbit online that I think both perfectly describes the roller coaster of emotions authors have about their creative process and also extends into how they feel about their books once they're out in the world:

This is awesome.
This is tricky.
This is shit.
I am shit.
This might be okay.
This is awesome.

That writing a book is so highly emotional, and that we put so much of ourselves on the line while we're doing it, makes it both fulfilling and agonizing. Writers willingly subject themselves to a process that is soul-baring and therefore enlightening in many ways, and yet nothing short of gut-wrenching because of all the possible emotions the act itself forces us to face.

On one call I had with an author I've worked with, I was reminded of how much we doubt our own capacity, often especially when the book is getting closer to being a reality. I was advising this author about how many books she should print as we approached publication. In order to benefit from economies of scale, and because she was printing a four-color art book, she needed to print one thousand books to make her investment worthwhile. Authors are a funny bunch in terms of expectations. While some are undaunted by the prospect of trying to sell one thousand books, to the point of thinking doing so should be almost easy, this author was ready to throw in the towel. I coached her through a few scenarios and talked to her about ways to leverage her book sales: she might teach classes and give away her book as part of the class; she might affiliate with other artists and sell her book directly at a steep discount; she might research partnerships—I named off at least three I could think of on the spot—and sell her book in bulk. At the end of our call, instead of feeling as if any of my suggestions was a viable option, the author told me she wished she'd never decided to publish her book.

Her reaction didn't catch me off-guard, only because I'm intimately familiar with the Author Freak-out Zone, the place authors typically enter once their book is in production. Red lights and sirens start going off in the Author Freak-out Zone anywhere from three to four months prior to publication, when the prospect of the book's being out in the world starts to feel very real. My client's reaction was undoubtedly prepublication jitters, as she eventually came around. But when you green-light your own work, it can be a lot more difficult to rally when things are looking bleak. You may become consumed by regret, thinking about what else you might have done with your money, besides having sunk it into your creative project. But this is the rub, and the focal point of this chapter. If you're treating your book like a baby, you're going to sink into despair fairly easily when something in the process catches you by surprise. The mentality of "book as baby" makes you less resilient because emotionally you're not thinking about all the ways in which your book is supposed to work for you, to carry its own weight, to do work in the world. It's good to love your book and feel proud of it but also to understand what it's for. It's a door-opener, a tool, and a product.

If you're under any illusion that you publish a book and then sit back and watch the sales roll in, or that someone will magically "discover" your work and propel you to the bestseller list, you probably need to have a heart-to-heart with a few other authors who've been through the publishing process. No author gets to sit back in this way; in fact, once the writing is complete, the hard work really begins. In order to publish well, you have to be in the driver's seat, eyes wide open, anticipating what's coming, which entails your getting creative (and working tirelessly) in the realms of self-promotion, marketing, and sales opportunities. Some authors are surprised to discover that their finished product is really just the first piece of a larger puzzle, but thinking of it like this from the get-go will help you to have a much more positive overall publishing experience.

One of my aims in this chapter is to help you to stop thinking of your book as your baby and to start treating it more like a product. The problem with the book-as-baby orientation to your project is that too often it gets in the way of your doing what you need to do, which is to try to be more objective so you can do the hard work of promoting and selling it.

Consider the following author personalities, which highlight some of the problems inherent in the author-as-parent concept:

Overbearing: These are writers who revise and revise and revise and are still working on their revisions ten years after they started. They are effectively smothering their project by not letting it breathe. When and if the book does come out, they're nervous Nellies, and usually down on themselves and the book: It could have been better. They could have done more.

Neglectful: These writers, by contrast, think they don't need to do much to get published. Writing a book is easy! They dash it off and barely care to get it edited. Publishing is easy! They slap on an unprofessional cover and have no qualms about self-publishing an inferior project. When their books come out, they're often totally shocked by negative feedback, and, depending on their personality, they either buck up and fix it or get defensive and blame the whole thing on the industry.

Self-conscious: These writers care deeply about their book, but they just can't bring themselves to talk about it with anyone. They don't want to work on their platform, for fear of sounding like a braggart, and they don't know how to toot their own horn, so, even if their book does make it into the world, it's at a severe disadvantage because the author would rather stick a fork in their eye than self-promote. The best of these authors get over it and allow their work to shine because they believe in it, but the orientation toward their project can be and often is legitimately damning.

Elitist: These writers think their book is the bomb—deserving of everything it gets and more. Their expectations about what their book can do are usually sky-high, and they're typically dumbfounded by their sales results, even if those are decent, because nothing but best-sellerdom was ever going to do. They secretly believe their book is better written, smarter, and more interesting than other people's books, and they want to be acknowledged for it.

The goal you strive for as an author should not be the same you'd strive for as a parent. You are your book's creator, so taking genuine pride in the work and in its publication is to be expected. But you need to gain some perspective about a) what's possible for a first book in the first place, b) how to leverage your book to make it work for you, and c) what it really takes to stay fresh and relevant out in the world once your book is complete.

Your book, as I said, is a door-opener. It can and will bring you unimaginable gifts—and eventually even gains. Remember how I said the completion of your book is just the first piece of the larger puzzle? I hope this chapter will offer you more pieces to consider to complete the mosaic of authorship, which entails holding on to your passion for your project but also understanding that the role of author intersects much better with that of businessperson than it does with that of parent.

Why to Treat Your First Book as a Freshman Effort

Aspiring authors can set themselves up for disappointment for a number of reasons, ranging from too-high expectations to a lack of understanding of the business of publishing to a flat-out misperception of what "good" sales actually look like. Writers want to publish for a lot of different reasons. For many writers, publishing a book is a longtime goal, a bucket-list kind of endeavor. Many people write to help others, just as many write because they can't *not* write. Not writing to these passionate writers feels like not breathing, and when a person feels that way, they're generally fairly prolific by default. There are plenty of aspiring authors, too, who want to publish to make money, or maybe for the validation, or sometimes even for the possibility of being famous. Money, validation, and fame are not bad goals in and of themselves, but if any or all of these are your goals— and whether you express them openly or furtively—you need to understand how unlikely it is that you will make money or get famous with a first book. The real money and fame in book publishing comes to those authors who work at their craft tirelessly, relentlessly, and over many years, as we touched upon in Chapter 3, in discussing the virtues of patience.

As a result, you should view your first book as your foundation book, an introductory effort. Depending on your writing goals, there might be a "right" type of book for you to publish as your first one. For instance, if you're a nonfiction writer, you want your first book to be something fairly simple, a topic that you can build upon in future books. It shouldn't be overly complex, or your magnum opus. If you have a system or a teaching platform or a Big Idea, then your first book should lay the groundwork. Its purpose should be to put you on the map, not necessarily to try to encapsulate everything you know.

If you're a memoirist or a novelist, your orientation to your material will of course be quite different. You've lived your one life, and you have a story to tell; or, if you're a novelist, you've no doubt lived with your idea for a book for some time before you sat down to follow through on your commitment to write the thing. So there's no foundational work; there's just the work. And you write the book you have been longing to write. You write the best book you can write.

But here's the important part: don't let that single book be the only book you write. If you want to be a career author, your next book (and the next and the next book, too) should already be percolating. It doesn't mean you have to be drafting your next book while you're still finishing your first book, but you at least want to know that you're going to do it. Publishing one book is a bit like completing your associate in arts (AA) degree. It's a great accomplishment, one to be proud of, but no one with an AA expects to get hired for high-level work in their field of interest. You cannot become a tenured professor or get a complex engineering job or become a doctor with only an AA under your belt. Those positions go to people who've put in the time to get more advanced degrees. Your second book, therefore, might be the equivalent of your BA; your third is your master's; and then, finally, by the time you publish your fourth, you're getting your PhD, and that will be the point at which you will start to see real gains from all the work you've put in.

Many experts say the needle starts to move after the third book. This makes sense: you get your master's, you start to see some payoffs. But also consider this analogy carefully as a way of tempering your expectations about what you can hope to achieve with a first book. What can an AA really do for you in your industry of choice? If you want to achieve success—including validation, good money, and even fame—you must keep going. Keep your eye on the big picture, the long journey.

One of the tricky things about book publishing is that we all hear stories of first-time authors who hit it big. They have a breakout book or, through sheer force of talent, they garner a big advance and become one of the next hot literati on the scene. These crazy success stories have created a lottery mentality in book publishing, one that causes other authors to think, *Why can't that happen to me, too?* There's nothing wrong with letting these thoughts in, even cultivating them. Hey, I am a believer in manifesting! But—and this is a big but—you don't manifest in book publishing without putting a whole lot of time, effort, and (frankly) money behind your efforts. Wanting it badly enough is not going to make it happen.

All the authors I know who've made it to best-sellerdom were toiling away just like every other persistent author who came before them until their big break came. There are countless examples of authors like this, beyond Christina Baker Kline, author of *The Orphan Train*, whom I mentioned in Chapter 3, and Mark Nepo, author of *The Book of Awakening*, whose story I share in Chapter 9. Sue Monk Kidd wrote three spiritual memoirs about her experiences in contemplative Christianity before she hit the best-seller list with her beloved novel *The Secret Life of Bees* in 2002. Jonathan Franzen published two novels, *The Twenty-Seventh City* (1988) and *Strong Motion* (1992), as well as a literary manifesto for *Harper's* magazine (1996), before *The Corrections* (2002) made him a household name. Anthony Doerr had published a number of books, including a collection of short stories, a memoir, and another novel, before his second novel, *All the Light We Cannot See* (2014), became a *New York Times* best seller and won the Pulitzer Prize for fiction in 2015.

Most of the authors we hear about, and especially those authors who are household names or who've achieved near-deity status in their particular genre, did not experience overnight success and did not become best-selling authors with their freshman effort.

Another important but simple part of this idea—that in order to succeed, you have to write more books—is that you have to publish. It doesn't matter who publishes your freshman effort, only that it's published well. It matters not that you publish with a traditional publisher or that you get an advance or have the right agent or editor. What matters is that the book is your best effort, that it has a killer cover, that it is designed per book publishing conventions and to acceptable standards— with all the right components—and that it be well edited (which usually means developmentally edited, line-edited/copyedited, and proofread).

The most successful authors I know (besides the handful of *New York Times* best-selling authors with whom I happen to be acquainted) are hybrid authors who publish traditionally and nontraditionally. This is because they own their process. They publish what they can with traditional houses, and they call the shots for everything else. These authors are the ultimate green-lighters of their work because they are not turning over their power to anyone. Phil Cousineau, author of many books, both traditionally published and self-published, picks and chooses the books he believes will have commercial appeal for the publishers and then publishes his own passion projects, because he understands the limited vision of the publishing industry and its inability to support every project he wants to pursue. His thirty-plus published books have won countless awards, and he sees the highest merit as finding the right fit for his books. For him, some works are best served by being published with a traditional press, and for others it's proved to be far better to use his own imprint. He ardently believes that what's most important is to find out the best fit for each book we write.

Publishing guru Kristine Kathryn Rusch is another such example. She publishes under a number of pseudonyms and variations on her real name and is both traditionally and self-published. (She also writes a fantastic blog about the business of publishing that all indie authors should subscribe to.) Authors like these two don't stand for the long waiting periods imposed upon them when an agent can't place a book or when they know that they're doing something special or niche enough that they're better off doing it on their own.

The point here is that you cannot wait. Don't sit on your debut effort, waiting for someone else to say yes. I'm not suggesting you don't shop the work in an effort to get an agent or a publishing house interested in it, but my rule of thumb is that you should wait no longer than six months for someone to say no. If an agent or editor has your work for longer than that, they're not interested. Put a limit on how long you'll entertain traditional publishing in general, too. I recommend one or two years maximum. Consider that during that time, you could already have published and could have learned a great deal about writing, publishing, and yourself in the process. Then consider the trajectory of your writing career if it takes you ten years to publish each book. It will be thirty years before that needle starts to move, and by then you'll be too disheartened and tired to believe your efforts worthwhile.

Please keep in mind as you're reading here that this chapter is intended to be a loving shove toward thinking about being more prolific, but the extent to which you respond to this shove has to do with how much you care about being a career writer and making money (or achieving fame) from your book. If your reasons for publishing are different—legacy, bucket list, etc.—then don't feel pressured. Not everyone needs to get a master's or a PhD. Many authors also succeed as first-time authors, though it's not usually the kind of success people think of when they think of big book sales. Selling through five thousand copies of a book is a big success, for instance. Getting a review from one of the trade magazines on a first effort is a major coup. Seeing your name in print in a journal or magazine you've always admired is a win, and something that might have happened only because your book opened the door. With your first effort, no matter what, you own the title "author," and you get to decide what happens next.

How to Leverage What You've Got

Okay, so, you have a first book either in your future or under your belt. And even if we're thinking of it as a freshman effort, it should be your best freshman effort. This means, as I've already mentioned, publishing it "right." Again, this doesn't mean you have to publish with a big, prestigious house; it just means the book has to look so good that no one questions whether it came from a big, prestigious house.

Leading up to publication, authors who aspire to give their books the best possibility for success will gather and hire a marketing and publicity team. Some authors decide to approach this modestly, by which I mean less expensively. Let's face it—at the end of the day, marketing and publicity is all about budget and how much you're willing to allocate to this area of your publishing endeavor. Publishing well, it turns out, is really expensive, even for authors getting the full ride that traditional publishing offers. Don't think for one second that those authors at the height of their career aren't paying a publicist or some kind of marketing team to keep them current, even if they are benefiting from a bigger in-house marketing and publicity campaign than most authors could ever hope to see.

What should you realistically spend on a publicist, then? It varies, but, knowing what I know now from my years as publisher of She Writes Press and my time in traditional publishing prior to that, I'd say $5,000, at least. Many authors I work with spend much more than that. One of my traditionally published clients spent $45,000 on her publicity efforts for a single book, which involved building her platform, pursuing national media, working for a year with a publicist, and covering all the travel expenses for her book-related events. This is a huge number, obviously, and most people don't have the funds or the inclination to spend that much—but the point is that people *are* spending that much.

Even if your first book isn't likely to send you into the stratosphere and make you a household name, you still need to pay to play. I know, I'm full of harsh realities, but there's a silver lining here, which is that you can achieve what you want to achieve through hard work. That publishing can sometimes be a lottery ticket makes it something authors can't help but pin their dreams onto, but for those willing to work hard, spend enough on themselves to garner some legitimate publicity successes, and then keep their eye on long-term rather than short-term goals, success will come. A lot of the ways in which authors are successful today, however, are not through the traditional means of selling their books through bookstores. That piece just gives you some legitimacy and, for a lot of authors, fulfills a lifelong dream. In fact, you have to leverage to be successful, and that means understanding how to do it and then working hard and following through on each of these kinds of opportunities:

THE THREE MAJOR SALES CHANNELS

Publishing expert Brenda Knight has a theory that if you pursue one of these three outlets, you could have a best seller on your hands, and if you pursue two, your book will be a success. They are: 1) trade markets; 2) special sales/mass markets, which include big-box stores, grocery sales, and specialty retail shops, like Urban Outfitters, and even retail stores with a specific focus, like Home Depot; and 3) e-books. The fourth and fifth areas of sales, which to Knight are just gravy, are foreign and audio.

So, how do you start to think about sales to these major outlets? Even if you have a publisher, you can be doing what Knight calls "augmentation without alienation." If you're self-published, it's all on you and your publicity/marketing team. Augmentation without alienation acknowledges that you have a publisher and/or a sales force that potentially holds the account that you are calling up or reaching out to. You pursue these leads by sending the account (i.e., the specialty gift shop or grocery store) a physical copy of your book, along with a note that says something to the effect of, "I'm sure you received this from my publisher, but I'm sending you another copy to make sure you have it, and because I believe that my book would be a good fit for your store." Then you detail the very specific reasons why your book would be a good fit. Match your message to the account's vision or mission statement.

This kind of outreach can go one of two ways. If the account likes your book, they might find your outreach refreshing. They rarely hear from authors, especially from authors who have business savvy and know what they're doing. It is unlikely that your effort will backfire, but if you don't hear back, you might do just one more follow-up before giving up. You don't want to become a stalker.

If you're a self-published author, you will need to be ready to fulfill these orders if you get a bite. This usually means being able to print upwards of five hundred to six hundred copies and fulfilling exactly how the account wants the books to be received. You can risk having all the quantity sent back if you don't adhere to their exact packing requirements and measurements, so pay close attention. If you get a bite from a retailer like this, congratulations. It may be possible to negotiate a nonreturnable sale, so vie for that as a first choice. If they ask for the books to be returnable, you need to decide whether you're willing to take this risk. Book publishing is a returns-based business, as we'll discuss in Chapter 6, so some accounts may insist that this is the industry standard, and you'll need to decide whether the sale is worth the risk of quantity coming back.

DIRECT SALES OPPORTUNITIES

Direct sales include but are not limited to the special sales markets mentioned above. Outlets for direct sales opportunities include associations, corporations, nonprofits, government services, libraries, book clubs, schools, hospitals, home improvement centers, pet centers, garden supply centers, grocery stores, museums, state parks, zoos, truck stops, gift shops, and more.

Direct sales are a whole other ballgame and an entire area that is ripe for exploration, depending on the kind of book you have. The trick with direct sales is to think broadly about the potential reach of your book. Direct sales opportunities are both nonretail and retail, but the holy grail is in nonretail because those sales are nonreturnable. If you're going to go after a retail account and you have a distributor, you need to consider Brenda Knight's advice above about augmentation without alienation. But if you're going after a nonretail account, your distributor (and, by extension, your publisher) is out of the picture, so you can sell directly and get a pretty nice profit out of the sale.

I experienced the power of a direct sale when a nonprofit organization called Now I Lay Me Down to Sleep purchased three hundred copies of *Three Minus One*, an anthology I coedited with director Sean Hanish. NILMDTS is a courageous organization that provides photography services to families who've lost infants. Our anthology, inspired by Sean's movie *Return to Zero*, on the subject of the stillbirth of his son, was in alignment with this organization's mission, and they wanted to use our book in their gift baskets to grieving parents. Beyond being quite touched by this purchase and knowing we were reaching parents struggling to make sense of their loss, we experienced this as a great direct-sale relationship. The organization was a nonprofit, made the purchase directly, and paid for the shipping. In this case, we sold our book at a 50 percent discount and paid only our manufacturing costs.

This example showcases the importance of understanding your audience. You want to reach out to negotiate a potential direct sale only if you know that the store, organization, association, or company you're reaching out to has a strong need for your book, or that the message or information in your book is a great fit for the population that outlet serves or sells to. Many She Writes Press authors have negotiated direct sales with corporations where they do speaking gigs. Sometimes a keynote or other speaking engagement can involve giving everyone a free copy of your book, which might be either bundled into your speaking fee or purchased by the corporation in advance.

Brian Jud, author of *How to Make Real Money Selling Books* and president of the Premium Book Company, which sells books on a commission basis to nonbookstore buyers, has graciously given me permission to share this chart he created, which shows the two sides of special sales marketing—retail and nonretail. Pay attention to the fact that nonretail involves contacting buyers. You are in charge here, and in most cases it behooves you not to bring in your distributor or publisher (if you have one). But in general, the nonretail system makes a great deal more sense. The contract buyers are buying in books they really want, based on concepts they think they can sell. On the retail side, the distribution drives books into the marketplace. Retail buyers make buys based on comparative titles (meaning sales of similar books) and on publishers' publicity goals and promises. I definitely put my bet on the nonretail side to sell more effectively.

To be successful and prolific at direct sales takes a lot of work and an unfailing belief that your book is going to speak to the particular audience of the organization you're selling to

Two Parts of Special Sales

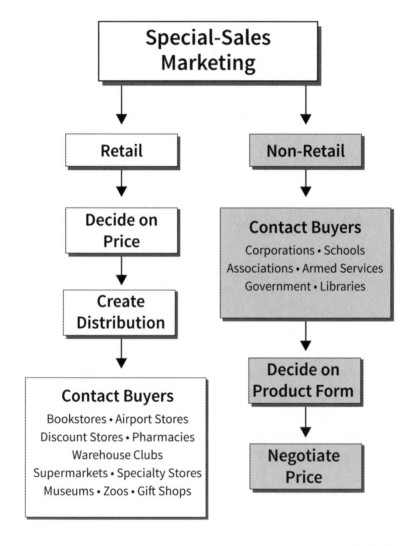

Special-Sales Marketing

Retail

Non-Retail

Decide on Price

Contact Buyers
Corporations • Schools
Associations • Armed Services
Government • Libraries

Create Distribution

Contact Buyers
Bookstores • Airport Stores
Discount Stores • Pharmacies
Warehouse Clubs
Supermarkets • Specialty Stores
Museums • Zoos • Gift Shops

Decide on Product Form

Negotiate Price

© Brian Jud

or be directly aligned with the customers of the particular store you're selling to. Direct sales work really well when the mission of your book is aligned with the mission of the nonretail outlet you're selling to. Thus, doing some research to figure out what these outlets are is worthwhile. Depending on your book's content, you may also want to explore Brian Jud's website, Book Marketing Works, to take a look at the services he offers to authors interested in maximizing their nonbookstore sales. Typically, nonfiction does better in nonbookstore markets because they're so specialized, but if you have very topical or issue-driven fiction, you might want to give it a whirl and see what the possibilities are.

LICENSING AND SUBRIGHTS

Many authors are understandably concerned about keeping their rights, doing due diligence and negotiating their contracts to retain subsidiary rights to their work . . . and then they do nothing with those rights. Depending on what genre you're writing in, it might be difficult to license your work, but most authors don't even try. An author with a typical publishing contract has licensed to their publisher the right to publish and distribute print and digital versions of their book, usually in a single language. In contracts with American publishers, the publishers retain either world or North American rights to sell your book. If your publisher is keeping world rights, they have the right to distribute the English-language version of your book internationally; it does not mean that they are necessarily invested in selling your foreign rights.

Most small publishers today don't have the bandwidth to deal with all the many possible licensing opportunities that exist for an author, so authors would do well to keep all of their sub-rights, unless their publisher has a plan in place to actively try to sell. A good time to start thinking about licensing is when your book is about six months to a year old. At this point, your marketing and publicity plan will have run its course. This can be a great time to do an audio version of your book to give the paperback and e-book versions new life. Any new variation on the original that you create gives you a new reason to talk about and promote your book.

In the preceding chapter, I mentioned Dean Wesley Smith and his magic-bakery analogy. Each piece of magic pie is a licensing agreement, and the pie itself has unlimited numbers of slices. One book is one piece of pie, with unlimited possibilities for portioning it off into slices that include things like an audiobook; foreign-language editions; rights to a game; movie or television rights; and excerpting portions of your work to other content providers, such as magazines, newspapers, and even other book publishers.

Once an author begins to harness the power of the magic-pie metaphor, they're likely to want more. And this is where many authors have become truly successful from a financial standpoint, because the bakery is full of pies—your inventory of multiple published books—and each of those books has innumerable licensing opportunities. We're going to talk about the power inherent in becoming a content monster below, but there's no question that thinking of your output (your content) as a money machine requires a major shift of perspective for many writers—especially those still stuck in the book-as-baby mentality.

Once you have six, seven, or eight pies, your magic bakery can and will be a real source of income for you. However, you have a lot to learn if you want to do this well. You need to be persistent and to have the capacity and the energy to look for licensing opportunities. But dedicating yourself to the research of finding the right relationships and pitching your work could pay off quite handsomely and could serve the purpose of keeping your existing book, and eventually your backlist books (titles that are four to six months past publication), alive.

Become a Content Monster

A lot of people want to know if there's a secret formula for publishing success. There isn't. Because authors invest in themselves at She Writes Press, many come into the endeavor with an expectation that they will earn out their investment. They're approaching the business of publishing with an entrepreneurial mindset and appreciate a model like ours, which gives back such high percentages of proceeds to the authors on the tail end. And while some do earn out, others do not. In this way, our model looks like every other model of book publishing, in which some books excel and earn out and some don't.

Keeping your focus on your book as product can help you be more proactive about the financial side of this business you've entered into. The profit margins on a single book are ridiculously small, even under a hybrid model, where authors keep a higher percentage of their royalties. You're looking at anywhere from under $1 per book to maybe $3 or $4 maximum, depending on your production costs and the publishing model you choose. For every publisher that exists, there are books that exceed expectations, books that perform to expectation, and books that lose the publisher money. If you're green-lighting your own work, you need to know that this is the case, that there is not a single publishing "solution" out there, and that this entire venture is not clear-cut or easy.

Understanding that you're peddling your particular wares—which happen to be content—can be kind of like a guiding light to you as you think about your priorities during and after publication. Content is actually the key to your ongoing and future success. It is the magic bullet, if there is one. Authors sometimes think that writing their book is enough—and it might be, if your only goal is to have a published book to your name. After all, it's hard to bang out eighty thousand words and then to do that again and again and again. Once you write your book and are in the throes of your publicity campaign, you're then supposed to write more and more content—guest posts and opinion pieces and your own blog posts and social media posts and articles, and the list goes on and on—because that's what keeps you fresh. People want more and new content, so this is what it takes if you're truly envisioning having a career as an author.

I call this section "Become a Content Monster" because, just as I confessed that I aim to help you to start thinking of your book as a product, I also aspire to help you to start mining your depths and your curiosity for content. You need to envision yourself as a bottomless well. You can never run out of things to write about, just as you can never run out of things to think about. The trick in becoming a content monster, growing your platform, and promoting your book(s) is to be on point with your content.

It takes a heck of a lot to become a content monster. Here's a snapshot of what they do:

1. They write at least three to four times a week (often more).
2. They have at least two books in progress, and they're actively working on at least one of those.
3. They write new content—blog posts or articles—at least once a month, usually more than that. Blogger content monsters often blog as much as once a day. These are supermonsters.
4. They post on at least two social media platforms every day.
5. They create cross-platform/multimedia content.
6. They know how to repurpose, which we'll get to in a moment.
7. They publish.

I want to qualify #7 here because you can obviously be generating tons of content and not be publishing, but the point of becoming a content monster, and really owning it, is to allow other people to read your work. This is part of treating what you do as a business and thinking of your book as a product. You don't get to call yourself a content monster if you're scribbling two thousand words a day in your journal. This is a great practice, but the aggressive awesomeness of content monsters is that they're generating stuff that other people will read. They're working their magic every day through the hard work of putting out content, creating visibility, and engaging readers with their work. This is another secret that all successful authors understand: you have to engage. Authorship is not just about putting out a book every so often. You also need to be actively engaging with a readership, which is why having a database and e-mailing your subscribers matters, as does having a website that you update regularly (usually through blogging) and being active and consistent on social media.

Creating content is not limited to writing. Look back at #5. What the heck is cross-platform/multimedia content? You might call it something different, but this is the kind of content I'm talking about:

1. audio/podcasts
2. electronic books
3. free reports/giveaways/drip campaigns
4. webinars/classes
5. conferences/events

And then there's #6—repurposing. Repurposing is taking content you already have and using it for another purpose. For example, I've repurposed content to write this book. (See the copyright page for acknowledgment.) Repurposing is pretty awesome once you get the hang of it, because it's a huge time-saver. I repurpose every day, actually, in that I extract the content for my social media posts from my blog posts. This allows me to parcel out social media content that I've already written, and it saves me the effort of always having to come up with fresh new ideas for Facebook and Twitter.

You can also repurpose parts of your book and sell them (as we talked about in the licensing section). This happens all the time when memoirists and novelists sell parts of their books to be included in an anthology. Sometimes the author has to slightly alter their work in order to make it fit the parameters of the anthology, which is why this is repurposing, and sometimes you'll see a disclaimer or credit line in an anthology that says something to the effect of, "The original version of this essay was published as a chapter in the author's memoir."

If you love to write and feel like you can pour endlessly onto the page, you may well already be a content monster who just needs to funnel your efforts into doing more active publishing, even if it's just on your own blog and social media. If you are a published writer who struggles with a tortured writing process, then nothing about what I'm proposing is going to feel easy. It may well be impossible, in fact. I've worked with talented writers over the years for whom every finished chapter of a book was like climbing Mount Everest in the dead of winter without the right gear. Some writers are spent and exhausted by the sheer effort of putting their words on the page, no matter how drawn they are to write. If you recognize yourself here, try baby steps. Try to adopt a discipline of blogging once a month, or posting something on one social media outlet once a day. Part of endeavoring to become a content monster, even if you end up becoming only a content shark, is creating a routine you can stick to and getting your writing out into the world in a meaningful way.

Stamina for the Journey

If this chapter knocked the wind out of you a little bit, come back to it later and reread it after you've had some time to digest what I've laid out. Getting clear on what it takes to become a successful writer may well help you figure out whether you really want to become a career author after all, or whether you have the stamina to reach for the goal you've set for yourself—to become an author with a fan base and a following eagerly awaiting your next installment.

On the flip side, I hope this chapter will temper the expectations of first-time authors so that they understand and equip themselves for the long road ahead. Knowing that the first book you put into the world is staking your claim to authorship can be a helpful thing, too, in that you can steel yourself a bit against what's coming. I always use the metaphor of a marathon to describe writing and publishing a book, and to run a marathon, you have to have a tough-as-nails mentality. It's about more than just the training, just as publishing a book is about more than just writing a book and becoming an author is about more than publishing a book.

I also want to encourage authors not to wait to publish! This brings us back to the overarching theme of this book. Many of you will come to a point where you will green-light your own work. Some of you will come to this decision easily, and others of you will have gone through the wringer before you're truly ready. Let any feedback you've gotten from agents or editors fuel you. If you've been told that your manuscript needs work, hire an editor to help you get to the finish line. If you've gotten the frustrating input from agents and editors "We love your book, but we just don't think we can sell it," let that, too, be something that fuels you. There is a readership for your book, and you need to get that first book out to learn what it means to be an author and then to decide what kind of author you're going to be.

Finally, if you've been coddling your book baby, or if you recognize yourself in those parenting archetypes at the beginning of the chapter, start shifting your approach to your work. If you can't stop using pregnancy and/or birthing metaphors in your language, that's okay—I'm not going to police you. But do start thinking of this thing you're creating as something that will bring you fans and earn you money and that requires a very specific kind of attention—that is not the parenting kind. Take genuine pride in your work, and try to avoid dismissing and/or criticizing your work at all costs. Learn how to talk about your book in a way that engages others. Speak about it from the vantage point of ideas, rather than what you've accomplished.

Also consider this question: How will your book serve others? It doesn't matter which particular goal you choose: to be supportive, entertaining, titillating—it's all fair game. But you want to figure this out early, because this is what gets people interested, and it's how you engage. Fully embracing that you've written something that you want not just to sell, but to sell the heck out of, and that you hope will be a vehicle for future success, is a good thing. You've created a product. Now own it.

Chapter 6.

What You Need to Know About Data and Distribution

Data and distribution may not seem intimately connected, but they are. Understanding your data and what choices you're making impacts your book's distribution and discoverability (the topic of Chapter 8). I want to preface this chapter with a request, which is that you hang with me through this chapter. We've covered a lot already, and this chapter is the densest and most information-packed chapter of the book, but data and distribution are likely the aspects of book publishing that most authors least understand. Authors who unlock the power of data and distribution are light-years ahead of authors who don't, and knowing what this stuff is all about is empowering, because you'll be able to troubleshoot problems, experiment with your data to garner better search results, and know how to talk to key industry decision-makers about carrying your book.

The goal of this chapter is to make data and distribution accessible. We're going to wonk out a little, but I promise to make it worth your while. By the end, you will likely be surprised by how much data you have connected to a given book project. If you're a self-published author, you're responsible for managing your own data, but if you're publishing with a press that has its own distribution, the press is responsible for uploading your data. This is an important distinction, and it's another area where distribution and data are connected. Any publisher with a traditional distribution system will manage its authors' data, and authors who try to manage it on their own will be working at cross-purposes with their publisher. So you also want to understand your distribution relationship before you start going crazy making data changes. I'm also going to explain why distribution is a game-changer—and why in today's book publishing climate, the single biggest thing that sets authors apart from one another is not whether they're self-published or traditionally published but whether they have access to traditional distribution.

The Power of Good Data

The book publishing industry is built on data. This includes everything you can possibly think of that defines or qualifies your book: your trim size, price point, categories, keywords, descriptive content, cover image, and on and on. We're talking about any bit of data you see when you look at a book listing on Amazon.

You might have come across the word "metadata" in your research about book publishing. Metadata simply means "data about data," and it's a way of referring to the collective data *about* a book, not the data or information that's *in* a book. Data is easy enough to gather and organize in itself, but between the amount of information attached to each book and the huge number of distribution channels responsible for picking up that data, the probability that your data will contain an error or an inconsistency is basically 100 percent. The metadata spreadsheets She Writes Press submits to Ingram for our titles have sixty-two columns of data points! We don't fill out every column for every book we publish, but the point is that that's a whole lotta data for any given title.

The reason metadata is misunderstood has more to do with writers' discounting its importance or failing to understand how the industry uses it than anything else. If you do a Google search on the topic, you'll see that every expert on the topic says the same thing: it matters—a lot. Plus—added bonus—Googling the word "metadata" is an experiment in interacting with metadata, as you'll witness firsthand how search engines use metadata to help you find what you're looking for. In a blog post on Joel Friedlander's TheBookDesigner.com, Betty Kelly Sargent writes about the advent of computers and their impact on metadata:

> "We had to help [computers] by figuring out a way that electronic data could be structured and transmitted in a consistent manner so that it could be easily received, interpreted, displayed, and stored without much interference from us humans. Hence, modern metadata. Since we humans give the computers the information they need to create the metadata, we are ultimately responsible for its quality."

The quality of metadata is both what matters and what often gets compromised. Authors often rush their metadata, treating it like a dreaded homework assignment, rather than what it actually is: a wand that enables them to more deeply penetrate the vast sea of data that lives out there on the Interwebs. The more data you can attach to your book, the more likely you are to be found. It's kind of like sending out a positive SOS signal online: *I'm here! Find my book!*

You want to treat your book data more like an online dating profile than like a homework assignment. Think about the kind of person you want to read your book. Imagine creating content around your book that will attract that person. Spend time with this exercise, and also don't worry about everything needing to be perfect, because you can always make changes later. The great thing about data is that it's constantly in flux and it's updatable. The only downside is that it's not always updatable overnight. For most publishers who are required to update their data through their distributor, changes generally take up to ten days. So this gives you incentive to get it as right as you can the first time.

Your metadata includes but is not limited to:

Title
Subtitle
Author
ISBN
Price (in multiple currencies)
Trim size
Format
Cover image

Page count

BISAC/Category

Keywords

Long description

Short description

Audience

Blurbs

Now, some of this data is more straightforward, while other data sends authors through the roof as they try to wrap their mind around what they're supposed to do. In my experience, authors struggle the most with BISAC/category and keywords. The reason the BISAC/category data stumps people is that this is a piece of data that differs depending on whether you're self-published or published on a press that's working with a distributor. If you're self-published, you choose categories through the platforms you're using to get published (like CreateSpace or IngramSpark). If you're working with a publishing company that has a distributor, you will be forced to choose BISACs, which are limiting to the point of being frustrating yet are so critical to a book's success that the marketing director at Seal Press once told me that a book's BISAC categories are as important as a person's gender. In short, you don't want to get it wrong. That's a lot of pressure!

Why is it this important? Because data identifies what your book is to its intended audience. Data is what directs your book to particular shelves—virtual and brick-and-mortar. If you get your BISACs/categories wrong, people coming to find a book on the topic you've written about may well overlook your title because it's not properly listed. This happens all the time!

For publishing houses, BISACs also determine which book buyers a given title goes to. If you're in the wrong category, it can be confusing to the buyer and can result in a pass.

After BISACs/category, keywords are the next-least-understood piece of data. You are trying to identify the keywords that people would enter into their search engine if they were looking for the topics or issues your book covers but didn't know your book exists. You want to try to think broadly, globally, and like your audience when considering what words or combination of words such people might use. Every book has up to seven keywords specifically associated with it, but keywords can also be embedded in your descriptive content and blurbs as well. Keywords are just words people are using to search. It's simple but also profound.

Amazon has an article you can Google called "Make Your Book More Discoverable with Keywords," a kind of best-practices approach to this particular metadata point. The article specifically notes that "relevant keywords can boost your placement in search results on Amazon.com." Google has a keyword tool you might want to play around with here: www.googlekeywordtool.com.

If you end up with a publishing house, your metadata will be collated into something called a tip sheet that your sales team will use to sell your book to accounts. The same metadata populates your Amazon, Barnes & Noble, Kobo, iTunes, and iBookstore pages. If it's pushed out through a large feed (which it will be if you are with a publisher that has a traditional distribution process), your data will go international, to hundreds of distribution partners, including places like Target, Fred Meyer, Walmart, and other superstores that simply make available books that are listed online. Getting this kind of far-reaching access is a great thing for most authors, but it's also where metadata starts to get messy. Even with one point of entry, metadata has a high probability of errors. Some retailers mess up data links in translation and fail to pick up changes; many have problems with their own systems or codes that result in broken links or bad characters. If you have more than one point of access or more than one person making changes to your metadata, mistakes are inevitable. Because metadata is often hand-entered as HTML code, human error is the biggest issue. Metadata can be a real thorn in the side of publishers and authors alike, who want it to be perfect and who run up against the limitations of perfection across hundreds of retailer access points.

Keeping your data up to date and error-free can be a full-time job, and that brings me back to my broader point to do it as right as possible the first time. Take time. Don't be hasty. Hire someone to proofread your content and double-check all your data points. I can't tell you how common it is to input varying price points across two different platforms—$15.99 one place and $16.00 somewhere else—or to inadvertently enter variations on a subtitle, or to forget to update a cover file when a change has been made. The list goes on and on. Have a master document where you keep all the specifics of your book's metadata and update it when things change. This should act like a password. It's specific and case sensitive and should be consistent wherever your book data can be found online. And when you find errors—and you will—don't freak out. Just get 'em fixed and keep monitoring.

Distribution Defined

Now let's turn to distribution, the method by which your book gets to wholesalers and retailers. Because there are so many channels, and because the line between distribution and fulfillment is blurry to a lot of newbie publishers and authors alike, people are often misinformed about what type of distribution they have or what it's actually doing for them. Another complication has to do with Ingram itself, a massive wholesaler that also happens to be a distributor.

When I started She Writes Press in 2012, my own understanding of distribution was based exclusively on traditional publishing. After all, I'd only ever worked for traditional publishers, so I took distribution for granted. When you work with a traditional distributor, a third-party company with a sales force and a title management system, it's kind of like having a machine at your fingertips; all you have to do is keep feeding it. Books are made available everywhere books are sold, and you don't have to track multiple systems to discover the root of a problem. It's all handled through your distributor, your central command. It's not a perfect system, but it's effective and streamlined.

As a new publisher of a fledgling company, I signed on with a company whose CEO told me they were a distributor. Still not fully understanding the difference between distribution and fulfillment myself, I didn't ask clarifying questions. I didn't go into this relationship fully expecting the kind of services I'd known and experienced with Publishers Group West, the distributor I'd worked with for my entire thirteen years in publishing to date. I understood that we wouldn't have a sales force and that all of our books were going to be print-on-demand and therefore not warehoused. I did not expect, however, nor could

I have foreseen, all of the holes in the system, until we had a few books in print. Our "distributor" (which was really a fulfillment company) made mistakes here and there with our data, but that was not as big a problem as the fallout from She Writes Press not having traditional distribution. Our books were often out of stock on Amazon because we had no streamlined system for restocking them in a timely manner. There was no preordering function, so books weren't even available for purchase until publication day. Because we were doing exclusively print-on-demand through Lightning Source, our books were showing up as available only in a Tennessee warehouse, so bookstores in other US regions simply refused to order our titles. We were cutting consignment deals with bookstores and handling shipping and returns. It was a complete and immediate nightmare for me, having come from a world where someone else had always handled all these matters. I had started a publishing company to acquire great books, to focus on their editorial quality and design, and to provide an alternative publishing option for women authors. Now, all of a sudden, I was stuck in these ghastly details, spending way too much time on logistical issues and fielding freak-outs from authors.

She Writes Press published its first book in September 2012, and by March 2013 I was actively looking for a new distribution partner. Given the volume of titles we were publishing and our authors' high expectations, we knew that without a solution—and a fast one, at that—we weren't going to make it. The solution for us was traditional distribution. And while traditional distribution is not for everyone, for She Writes Press it's opened doors. It's increased our visibility, decreased the stigma (somewhat) of being automatically perceived as a "POD publisher" (more on this later as well), and legitimized our program within the industry.

The publishing industry is still very much an old boys' club, so when you green-light your own work, you need to understand what's going on with your distribution so that you can have conversations with bookstores and libraries and any other outlet where you want your book to be carried or made available. If you don't know what's happening behind the scenes, you will end up giving wrong or confusing information to the very people you're wanting to sell your book. I wrote earlier in this book about needing to treat publishing as more than a hobby if you want to do it right. At the very least, it should be a pursuit, if not a full-fledged business endeavor.

She Writes Press grew very fast, and within six months we had the kind of book inventory and quality that made us a good candidate to partner with a traditional distributor. Not every self-published author has that option. You typically can't get a traditional distribution deal unless you've published ten titles, or if your book is gaining so much traction that the distributor sees you as something of a sure bet—meaning that they can see that a lot of inventory is going to be flowing through. A traditional distributor will scrutinize your content and your presentation. If your covers and interiors aren't well designed, you may well never get a call back from a distributor you approach. It's not a shoo-in kind of situation, and there are few good alternatives, which is why distribution is a real pain point for self-published authors and is the biggest problem indie authors need to solve if we truly want to level the playing field.

I realized that for She Writes Press, traditional distribution was going to be a game-changer, and it has been—so much so that I've come to believe that the divide between traditionally distributed authors and everyone else is a bigger gulf than the divide between traditionally published and self-published authors. Indie authors want visibility, access, and legitimacy, and they deserve that. Making sure your book is easy to get, set at the right industry discount (55 percent), and returnable is key, but that's often not enough for a bookstore to want to carry a self-published title. I believe that one of the reasons hybrid publishing is such a viable solution for independent authors is that so many of these presses have access to traditional distribution, which allows bookstores to simply say yes and to order through your distributor. You step aside and let things play out. It's a system that's been in place for years and years and that everyone along the food chain understands. If you've experienced the kind of headache I did with my She Writes Press titles before we got traditional distribution, then you know well the pain points I experienced. You want to consider what kind of importance distribution is going to play in your next publishing endeavor and add this question to the mix as you deliberate your publishing options.

IngramSpark or CreateSpace: What's the Difference?

IngramSpark and CreateSpace are platforms, owned by Ingram and Amazon, respectively, that allow authors to self-publish. IngramSpark is a relatively new platform, created to replace Lightning Source, which many consumers thought was not as user-friendly as it should be. It's important to note that both IngramSpark and CreateSpace are in the business of printing. You can hire CreateSpace directly to produce your book. They offer comprehensive design and editing services, but that is not their primary business. CreateSpace also offers you the option to use their company as your publisher. *Do not do this.* Create your own imprint and upload your own independently designed files. Showing up in catalogs as a CreateSpace book is the kiss of death for you, as far as a lot of buyers are concerned. There are enough anti-Amazon bookstores out there that you don't want to hitch your wagon to Amazon as your publisher.

That said, it's fine to use CreateSpace as your printer. IngramSpark and CreateSpace are both on-demand printers that can print a single copy at a time, or thousands. Their rates are competitive with offset printers for up to five hundred copies, after which point it's more cost-effective to use an offset printer to print your book. But the value of print-to-order technology cannot be overstated, and most self-published authors should be using IngramSpark or CreateSpace to print their books.

The two companies' offerings are comparable. They're on par with each other in terms of their setup fees and print costs. In my own experience, Ingram has superior print quality. CreateSpace's primary asset is its relationship with Amazon. When you hire an Amazon company, your book's availability on Amazon is seamless, and since it's the retail outlet most authors care about, this is worth a lot. But if you're an author who isn't putting all of your eggs in the Amazon basket, Ingram's reach is much more extensive. They have more publishing partners and a broader distribution network. They also own their own wholesale company, Ingram Wholesale, which is an effective distributor of titles across many hundreds of potential accounts.

Both companies offer you what they call "extended distribution," which is, unfortunately, less effective than it sounds. Ironically, CreateSpace uses Ingram to distribute its own books beyond Amazon. That said, all "extended distribution" means is that your book is technically "available" to bookstores; it does not mean it's for sale or that it's easy to get. And if you have not done your due diligence and marked your book as 1) being at a 55 percent discount to the trade and 2) returnable, you can't even have extended distribution. These two things are deal-breakers for bookstores. Consider up front how valuable bookstores are in your sales-and-exposure equation. If the answer is "very," use IngramSpark and follow all its discounting and returnability rules. If the answer is "not very," then use CreateSpace, go ahead and set a lower discount (maybe 30 percent), and go full bore for Amazon sales above all else.

(continued on next page)

One side note here is that I've known authors who've uploaded to both platforms—to use Ingram for their distribution and higher-quality paper, and CreateSpace for their efficacy with Amazon. This seemed to work fine. CreateSpace fulfilled the Amazon orders, and Ingram everything else. The only downside here would be that you'd have print variations from platform to platform, and you'd have to pay two separate setup fees, and work with your designer to prepare your design templates as specified by each platform. But this might be something you want to experiment with, especially if you're torn over which company to print with.

A Deeper Look at Traditional Distribution

In this book, I've been using the term "traditional distribution" to describe the kind of distribution a publisher has when they sign on with a third-party distribution company as a publisher client. This is different from everything else, including fulfillment services and extended distribution through self-publishing houses, both of which are ineffective at getting bookstores and libraries to carry titles but fine for fulfilling retailer orders.

Distribution, like a lot of words in book publishing, is used to describe a process: the process by which books go from the printing plant to the retailer (in the case of print-on-demand) or from the warehouse to the retailer (in the event that inventory is being stored). But, as we all know, not all processes function the same way. Distribution channels exist to get books to customers, but the effectiveness of the systems built to make that happen varies a lot. The rise of self-publishing is responsible for the aforementioned confusion about distribution, because, as more and more self-published authors publish, "distributors" are springing up to meet the demand. The "distributor" (really a fulfillment company) that She Writes Press signed with during our first year of existence had nothing more than an account with Lightning Source. They were using extended distribution, just like any other self-published author, and had no reach into the marketplace with their own sales force or relationships. Once I stood back and realized what their role was—that of a middleman—I saw how much more effective it would be just to cut them out. The services they were offering were helpful, but we could have hired a single employee to do the same thing: enter metadata, upload files, and order books.

Had we not made the jump to Ingram Publisher Services (the traditional distribution arm of Ingram), we would have been better off having our own direct relationship with Lightning Source. This is a possibility for all self-published authors to consider. If you have or are thinking about having a middleman, why? What are they offering you that you can't do yourself, and are their services worth it? Are they taking a cut of your royalties to do finite and measurable work? If so, you might want to consider cutting them loose.

Traditional distributors do charge a fair amount for the privilege of distributing your books. They take a base, and a commission on top of that. For most authors looking to greenlight their own work and publish independently, the only way to get traditional distribution is to partner with a press that already has it. There are many deals to be made with publishers everywhere, by the way, so keep that in mind. It's not outside the realm of possibility that you would identify a publisher you think is a good fit for your book and then reach out to them and ask them if they'd be interested in a distribution relationship—where you pay them for their access. You have to know what you're asking for, of course. But I've coached authors through requesting a formal meeting with a publisher and talking over the possibility of cutting a hybrid deal with that publisher—paying for certain services in exchange for their distribution. You approach this like the business proposition it is, but it's important to know that these deals are happening all over the place. And, as I said earlier, if you really think your book has a chance of breaking out, you're going to need this relationship.

Here's what traditional distributors do for their publisher clients:

• **They presell publishers' books into major and small accounts.** They have a sales force that has relationships with book buyers. Those reps go out on monthly sales calls and individually sell titles to buyers. It's competitive, yes, but they get face time with buyers.

• **They collate, organize, and output metadata.** All traditional distribution companies have major platforms in place to collect data and then release it, via daily feeds, to retail channels like Amazon, Barnes & Noble, Kobo, iBookstore, IndieBound, etc.

• **They maintain relationships with major accounts.** Again, they have access to all the major retail outlets where you might otherwise find it impossible to reach an actual human.

• **They streamline processes.** This is way bigger than it sounds. The point here is that if a traditional publisher warehouses your book, there is a steady, stable pipeline from their warehouse to wholesalers and retail partners. They're shipping massive quantities of books every day. There will never be a delay in your order, and your book will never show up as being out of print—unless it really is. For anyone who's self-published and wondered why their book is showing up as low stock or temporarily unavailable on Amazon or any other retailer's website, it's because this pipeline has to be well oiled. My observation is that only traditional distributors have the right oil.

• **They have access to special sales accounts and libraries.** There are certain markets that self-published authors simply cannot penetrate—and these markets are among them. You cannot get your book into airport bookstores, Costco or Target, or libraries without traditional distribution. (Okay, yes, you might be able to get your book into a couple libraries, where you have connections, but this is not the same as being picked up broadly by the library system.) This happens partly because these buyers want certain guarantees—on pricing, on returns (though library sales are nonreturnable). They don't want any headaches, and they're unlikely to partner with self-published authors because it's too much of a gamble. You could say that it's a case of not wanting to deal with an unknown quantity, but that's their prerogative.

Now let's look at what you get with extended distribution, by comparison. There is no preselling. There is no collating or organizing of metadata. You do that yourself, although the platform you're working with (usually IngramSpark or CreateSpace) will indicate what fields you need to enter. They do output the data for you. With extended distribution, you will forge your own relationships with retailers. Some of those retailers are helpful, like Amazon. They'll answer the phone when you call. There are other retailers you will not have a chance in hell of talking to. With extended distribution, your experience is not streamlined, it's decentralized, but since most authors care only about Amazon, we can at least thank Amazon for being receptive to individual authors' concerns. Finally, extended distribution means you have no need for specific or special sales relationships. It's possible that libraries would order your book, but libraries aren't looking specifically to order independently published books.

The bottom line is that indie authors without traditional distribution are limited. It behooves you to figure this out before you publish. This information may even change your mind about how you were intending to publish. If you want real bookstore and library results, you need traditional distribution. CreateSpace's and Ingram's extended distribution is a start, but it's not a solution.

The Potential Fallout of Controlling Your Amazon Data Directly

Many authors I work with seem to care only about Amazon. It's the only account they consistently check, though sometimes to their detriment. If you are a self-published author, you manage your own metadata through your Author Central account, which you want to set up as soon as your book becomes available on Amazon.com. You need to "claim" your book, and then you have access to a control panel of sorts where you can enter in all sorts of data about it.

Be forewarned, however, that if you have a publisher or are partnering in any way with a publisher, your data entry will override theirs. This is a point of frustration for many publishers, because authors sometimes cannot help themselves. They get impatient and want to make their own changes directly. For She Writes Press authors, this urge has resulted in duplicate entries and lost data.

Before She Writes Press was traditionally distributed by Ingram, we had no way to make metadata changes on our authors' behalf; only the authors could make those changes. It was great for authors who wanted to control their own data, but as a publisher we felt impotent, unable to help our authors and further contributing to a lack of systems.

A friend and ex-colleague told me over lunch one day, "Amazon is author-friendly; they're not publisher-friendly." It dawned on me for the first time that day that Amazon actually

(continued on next page)

has an incentive to bar new publishing models from having easy ways to make changes to their metadata. After all, CreateSpace is a direct competitor to many indie publishing solutions. And Amazon is king, no doubt about it. Love 'em or hate 'em, you need them. Amazon, meanwhile, does not need publishers and in fact sometimes undermines them by being indispensible to indie authors.

Tend to your Author Central account as you wish, but consider your publisher before you make changes directly or call Amazon directly. And if your publisher tells you it will take ten days, give them the benefit of the doubt. On day ten, call your publisher if the data isn't updated. Going to Amazon at that point is like going to Daddy after Mommy told you to be patient. I understand the impulse, but remember Amazon's motivation for being so author-friendly, and know that you might have some metadata consequences as a result of your desire to work with them directly.

BOOKSTORES

If you don't have traditional distribution on your radar and you're going to publish through CreateSpace or IngramSpark, note these few things about being carried in bookstores. You're opting into extended distribution because of its promise to make your book *available* to retailers. But the problem is that this availability exists only in theory, and you have to play by the bookstores' rules. First, you must set the discount for your book as the standard 55 percent off. Then you must set your book to be "returnable." You then have the option to choose whether you want returned books to be delivered or destroyed. If you want them delivered, you will pay a processing fee and end up with returned books coming to your house. While destruction of inventory is a sad part of the business, it's a less expensive and less complicated alternative for most self-published authors.

Now let's consider bookstores and what incentive they have to order your book. The only reason they'll usually stock your book is if you're a local author, or maybe because you have local connections. You can walk into a bookstore and show the buyer there a copy of your book. If it's well done and you promise to drive people to their store, it's possible that they'll carry your book on consignment (and will generally pay you 50–60 percent of your list price on books they actually sell). Some bookstores, like Book Passage in Marin, California, and Elliott Bay in Seattle, are known to support indie authors; others simply don't have the interest or the bandwidth to do so.

Bookstore owners have a tough job. The margins on books are abysmal, online retailers are running them out of business, and books, because they're heavy, are more expensive to ship than a lot of other products. Bookstores have deals with distributors where they get free shipping, which gives them incentive to order. If they get free shipping and get to return inventory for free as well, they can find themselves in a fairly low-risk situation where inventory is concerned. I've had plenty of experiences with bookstore owners who flat-out refused to order books they couldn't get free shipping for, and while it's frustrating, it's economics and I'm not going to begrudge a small-business owner their frugality. So, as an author, you have to be nimble, whether you have books housed in a warehouse or not. You need to be prepared to sell your books directly on consignment and to eat the cost of shipping, both ways, if necessary. This is what it takes today to have independent bookstores carry and sell your book.

Some bookstores may ask you to pay a co-op fee, a charge for the privilege of having an event in their store. This usually runs around $50–200. Not all bookstores ask for that, but don't be surprised if they do. I once heard a joke at a publishing event that went, "If you want to make a million dollars in publishing, then spend $2 million." A bookseller is not your friend until you make their store money. Don't take it personally. Just show up, bring lots of people, and urge your audience to buy your book and support their indie bookstore. Part of thriving as an author is forging relationships, so knock the socks off your indie bookstore and you'll make a friend for life.

LIBRARIES

Libraries are like the holy grail of book sales. First, they're non-returnable sales, so that alone makes them a coveted sales channel. But for many authors—particularly literary novelists and memoirists—library sales also represent another form of legitimacy. To have a book that's good enough for libraries to carry it says something about what you've written. It will be in the stacks forever, available to the reading public. For many, this is a values issue. Many writers grew up going to libraries, and there's something nostalgic and special about the idea that your book might be carried there, especially in a major city library or system of libraries that might order multiple copies of your book to carry at all their sites.

Library sales happen through Baker & Taylor, a wholesaler that supplies libraries, among other accounts. As an indie author, you do have the possibility of getting your book into libraries, but, again, it's not going to happen on its own, solely because you published a book. As an indie author, you have to hustle all the time. If you want libraries to carry your book, you need to do the legwork yourself. You can send free sample copies (either advance reader copies or final printed copies) to librarians. It's possible to buy a list of librarians' names. You can take out ads in *Booklist* and/or *Library Journal*, though getting reviewed by those outlets is really what would trigger doing an ad in the first place. You can also try to go to the American Library Association's (ALA's) annual conference, which is touted as having superseded Book Expo of America in terms of its relevance and impact within the industry. But most self-published authors don't have the wherewithal or the finances to attend trade shows, which is another reason traditional distribution starts to look like such an advantage, since all these coveted relationships and ordering mechanisms are already in place.

What About E-books?

It's important to note that the main benefit of traditional distribution, truly, is for print books. Where e-books are concerned, you can set up direct relationships with e-tailers, like Kindle, Kobo, Nook, and iTunes. Authors who are focused on e-book publishing really don't need to worry about traditional distribution. Hugh Howey famously signed a "print-only" publishing deal with Simon & Schuster, retaining his digital rights. He did this because he knew that Simon & Schuster's print distribution was unrivaled but that by keeping his digital rights, he would make a lot more money and manage those retailer relationships directly.

At She Writes Press, we use Ingram Publisher Services for both print and e-book distribution because of the ease of having all of our metadata entered in one central database. Other publishers feel adamant about having direct relationships with e-tailers. Both systems work, and there are absolute advantages to the direct relationship. Working directly with e-tailers affords you more flexibility and speedier changes to metadata, but if you want to get your book on multiple e-platforms—like Kindle, Kobo, Nook, iBookstore, LibraryThing, etc.—consider hiring a data management company to streamline your metadata for you. A reputable company in the industry is Firebrand Technologies, which allows you to experience a single point of entry for metadata, like traditional distributors have. They have over two hundred trading partners, and if you're serious about self-publishing, this company can and will up your game.

Traditional Distribution's Achilles' Heel: Returns

The fact that books are returnable is cause for frustration among publishers and authors, and it should be cause for broader concern—from both a financial and an environmental standpoint. I know I've just spent this whole chapter convincing you that traditional distribution is better, but there's a dark underbelly to the entire process that authors need to understand, especially if they're the ones footing the bill.

Publishing is a returns-based industry, a holdover from the Great Depression. The story makes sense in the context of the era: Book sales were falling. Publishers came up with a solution: consignment, which basically equals guaranteed sales. Booksellers had to pay only for what they could sell and then returned the rest. The problem is that we never dialed it back, and nothing about the industry has changed in almost a century. The fallout, of course, is that retailers have little incentive to order what they think they can *really* sell, and publishers rarely push back on what might be perceived as unrealistic orders because they're desperate for a shot at getting their product in a position where it *might* move.

As a small publisher, I'm extra-cautious about Barnes & Noble and outright against being carried in superstores like Target, Costco, and Walmart. I once worked on a book that got a big Target buy: thirty thousand books at a 60 percent discount, meaning the publisher got to divvy up 40 percent with the author. Of course, the publisher did not pay the author right away for those sales. They had to do what's called "holding money against returns" because of the likelihood that

Target would return inventory. Well, guess how many came back? Twenty-five thousand books. Those books were a write-off for the publisher. Pulped. Destroyed. This little scenario did not put this publisher out of business, because they could absorb that kind of loss, but twenty-five thousand books would have cost the publisher in the ballpark of $20,000–30,000. My company is not in a position to take that kind of hit, nor is any individual author we work with, which is why I avoid any possibility for this type of massive and steeply discounted order. It can sink a small publisher and be devastating to an author.

Barnes & Noble isn't quite as bad as a superstore, but they still mostly take buys that they can't or won't sell through. ("Sell through" is the industry term for books that actually sell through the register, meaning a real sale.) It's maddening, because most authors want their books to be in B&N, and it's good for a book to have that "chance," but B&N's returns of a given title are often higher than 50 percent, when the industry standard is 30 percent. They're also notorious for sending back damaged books. At a panel I attended at the Independent Book Publishers Association's Publisher University in Austin, one of the presenters joked that the guys packing up the pallets run over them with their forklifts for good measure, but the joke landed a little too bitterly. All the publishers in the room were frustrated by the lack of accountability from anyone anywhere—bookstores, wholesalers, distributors—when it comes to damaged books. The publisher eats it. End of story. And returns are only slightly less frustrating than damaged books. Yes, they go back into inventory, but publishers pay for that privilege, and often we're left with more inventory than we can sell, which eventually turns into excess inventory, which we have to pay to store.

Until we can change the industry's standard operating procedure—though I'm not sure what it's going to take to do that—publishers and authors need to pay to play. Saying that you will not accept returns, or marking your self-published book as "nonreturnable," is the kiss of death for your book, because no bookstore will touch it and you'll look like you don't know what you're doing. Yes, the returns are painful. Authors are generally dismayed by the hold against returns on their royalty statements and then outright flabbergasted by the sheer volume of books coming back from accounts that never needed to have ordered them in the first place. But this is all normal, unfortunately. Even best-selling authors have huge returns coming back to publisher warehouses.

For now, the problem of returns is a known quantity that we all complain about but seem to be powerless to change. One of my hopes is that the rise of independent authors will eventually shift the balance, because they're more likely to point out the madness for what it is. We need to make room for new ideas, and I will be right in line with the rallying masses who are saying, *This makes no sense!* Authors and new publishers need to continue to be disrupters and to come up with viable solutions to this outdated problem. Eventually our voices will be collective, and loud enough that we'll effect real change together.

How We Might Fix the Returns Problem

The traditional distribution process, as it exists, does work, despite the frustration that returns cause. An individual distributor's capacity to sell books into accounts and fulfill those orders is the foundation of their business model, one that in itself is not broken. What *is* broken—and contributing to all those returns—is preordering. I'm not talking about individuals preordering on Amazon; I'm talking about retail accounts preordering quantities of individual titles, based ostensibly on what they think they can sell, and then returning what they don't.

What's disturbing about this way of doing business is that there is an alternative; it's called print-on-demand (POD). However, instead of rescuing the industry, POD has become synonymous with self-publishing and thus stigmatized to a nearly unshakeable extent, despite major improvements in POD technology. POD is a printing process, though not limited by any means to self-published authors. It's true only that most self-published authors don't start with offset printing (a process that uses a **photographic technique to transfer images from metal plates to paper**), while most traditionally published authors do.

Here are a few facts about POD:

1. It's used by self-published authors who don't want to spring for an offset print run of one thousand copies or more.
2. Traditional publishers use it for their backlists and to print emergency copies of titles that are selling better than expected and that therefore require a quick turnaround while the publisher waits for their next offset-print run.
3. The print quality of POD has improved significantly in the past few years, so much so as to make POD books indistinguishable from offset-printed books.

If retail accounts ordered more conservatively and/or publishers stopped taking returns, we would have a viable solution to our wastefulness. Instead of printing thousands of copies to cover preorders, publishers would print more modestly, based on conservative sales estimates from retailers. They could and would still do offset-print runs for quantities exceeding one thousand, but they would have real incentive to move a POD book more quickly than they currently do.

If the stigma associated with POD books went away, bookstores would not be so resistant to ordering them. Today, bookstores still ask whether a book is POD, as if that's a reason for them not to carry a title. It's simply not. But because POD has become a euphemism for self-publishing, when a bookstore asks that question, they're really trying to weed out self-published titles. Some book buyers don't even understand what they're asking for when they ask if a book is POD; all they know is that POD causes them ordering problems. But that doesn't have to be the case if the self-published author offers to do consignment and to foot the shipping costs. Meanwhile, the industry subtly and actively works to marginalize self-published authors in order to assert its superiority, and using POD as a measure of a book's status is an easy way to do this.

When B&N goes out of business, as it eventually must, I desperately hope that book publishers will rally together to say "no more" to returns. Being a returns-based business is bad from every angle, and the damage to the environment should not be understated. We're printing more than we need. While books sit in retailers' warehouses, not moving, inventory must be available at the distribution warehouses to fulfill actual orders that *are* moving. This forces publishers to overprint, even publishers that are using POD technology.

Concerned publishers, authors, and readers can and should band together over this issue, but I fear that B&N would have to fall and Amazon would have to be reasonable (the prior an eventuality, the latter a near-impossibility) for us to make any headway in this area. Furthermore, traditional publishers would have to let go of their bias against POD. Certain bigger publishers could choose to be industry leaders on this point, trailblazing the way for others as we collectively try to reduce excess in this industry that relies on trees—a limited resource—to make its products.

Understandably, small bookstores will be upset by this shift, but they already order conservatively and their returns are already (generally) relatively low. Plus, they can do their part to reconceptualize the model. Independent bookstores and independent authors need to be forging better alliances, instead of acting as if they're cut from a different cloth.

Most indie authors will continue to use POD technology to print their books, and they should. I advise POD authors never to lead a conversation with how their books were printed. If you're talking to a book buyer, event venue, bookseller, conference organizer, or librarian, don't say anything unless they ask you. The book should speak for itself, so if you've hired a good design team, you should be able to present a product that you're proud of and that won't raise any eyebrows or set off any alarm bells (which can and will happen if your book "looks" self-published, meaning it has a subpar cover and/or interior design).

If you get into a conversation about POD, you can try to educate the person you're talking to, but this is uncomfortable territory for many authors—understandably. Still, your book shouldn't be prevented from being carried in bookstores as long as it's returnable and priced with the correct discount. Yet many bookstores have policies in place that make it difficult for POD authors to get their books in—even though this sometimes happens because employees are misinformed or don't know any better.

New publishing models, including hybrid models, will begin to replace old models, and eventually the big houses will start to see the value in the flexibility and smart economics these models embody (shared costs, better royalty scales for authors, and POD print runs).

But mostly, it's authors who will effect the change. They'll stop standing for being treated like second-class citizens. Those who will feel most empowered at first will be the hybrid authors, those who publish both traditionally and independently, because they have one foot in each world. And plenty of these authors are speaking out already. Second to them will be those authors who have rejected traditional deals to pursue alternative options for reasons of control, flexibility, and economics. And it will trickle down from there. POD should be treated for what it is—a valuable technology that prevents authors from printing more stock than they can sell. It says nothing about a book's merit, and the industry needs to stop propagating the myth that it does.

To succeed in this industry as an independent author, you don't need to be part of the old boys' club, but you do need to be able to hold your own, to push back when things seem unreasonable or unfair. The green-light crowd needs a club of our own anyway, where what's valued is not necessarily how things have always been done, but the standards we want to adhere to. And since the only standard in publishing is the gold standard, we'll continue to put out stellar metadata, created with tender loving care, and keep pushing on the distribution side until there are good and viable options for all authors.

The future of your book's success hinges on discoverability and availability, driven by data and distribution. As we reach the end of this chapter, you should be satisfied that you're in good shape with these two aspects of publishing, either because you have a handle on them or because you're working with a publisher who does. If not, I hope you have a fire in your belly to make some changes to give your current and future books a better chance at success.

Chapter 7.

Subverting the System
While Working Within It

What does it mean to be subversive? What do independent authors and publishers gain from being subversive? And, perhaps most important, do we need to be subversive in order to achieve our goals?

Per *Merriam-Webster*, "subversion" is "a systematic attempt to overthrow or undermine a government or political system by persons working secretly from within." It's quite an image, I realize, indie publishers working from within to overthrow or undermine—and so I'd like to clarify what I'm advocating for here. Traditional publishers today are working to actively separate indie authors from traditionally published authors. They do in fact have something to gain by keeping indie authors down, which is their supremacy in the industry. All publishers are deeply concerned with discoverability—how readers are going to find their books—but some traditional publishers (primarily the Big Five) feel as if indie authors and emerging publishing models are cutting into their market share. The industry is feeling the seismic shift I've been talking about throughout this book, but instead of finding ways to celebrate the best books, regardless of how they're published, it is pushing all the time for segregation.

I've mentioned some of these segregation efforts in earlier chapters—that indie authors are barred from many contests and not permitted to become members of certain associations; that indie authors are forced to submit to for-pay review outlets that have separate review sections for traditionally published authors, who do not have to pay. Certain big publishing houses even have policies in place that prevent their authors from endorsing self-published books! All of these efforts, which the industry defends unequivocally, point to a blatantly discriminatory system. When you find yourself in a system that is discriminating against you, you have two options: 1) simply deal with it, accept things as they are, and work your tail off, against the odds; or 2) refuse to put up with it, and advocate for the equal treatment you deserve.

This chapter focuses on how to advocate for equal treatment, which is subversive but also necessary and exciting. Independent authors today are change-makers, visionaries, and sometimes rebels. They're entering into publishing for all the same reasons authors always have: to spread a message, to be heard, to make money. I wrote in Chapter 1 about the 1 percent: the authors who get big advances, red-carpet treatment, and the kind of attention every writer dreams of to make their books a real success. The rest are the other 99 percent, who are a liability until they prove otherwise by making their house money. The irony of the way the publishing industry works is that the very people who are responsible for publishers' income—authors—are seen as a burden and often end up getting ignored, sometimes even treated quite badly, by their publishing houses. The mentality in publishing centers on finding something that sticks, and if a book doesn't stick in the first three months (sometimes even sooner than that), it's basically over. The author herself can promote and advocate for her own book, but the publishing house is largely done. Sometimes publishers handle this ending point with grace, sometimes not so much. When I was at Seal Press, we spent a great deal of time mulling over the best ways to talk to authors about "leaving the nest." Should this message come from the editor, who has the longest-standing relationship, or the publicist, or the head of marketing? We referred to it as a "come to Jesus" moment, when we were cutting the cord and the author had to deal with the fact that we'd done all we were going to be able to do for the book. Sometimes—oftentimes—this was astonishingly little.

It's important to note here that individuals—editors, publicists, marketing directors, publishers—often really do care about the books they've acquired. My critique of big publishing is not about the individuals but about a culture that is broken. When it comes to the biases against self-publishing that exist in these houses, I can almost hear the conversations: *Well, you don't want to be associated with a self-published author, so you probably shouldn't blurb that book.* They likely see this as a very valid separation, in an effort to protect their authors, but editors having these kinds of conversations are incredibly myopic, just like the industry they work in. Most editors working in traditional publishing have no idea what it feels like to be on the receiving end of a "no." They believe that they're curators, discerning the good from the bad. It's not until an editor has an experience like the one I shared in the introduction—of being gently advised against acquiring a book I championed and being met with enthusiasm about a book I knew to be subpar—that their worldview may begin to shift.

There's an all-encompassing buy-in that happens when you're immersed in a culture where everyone sees things the same way. It doesn't matter whether it's a religion or a political system or a family dynamic—in order to start to see differently, you must begin to question. And there are many, many people in traditional publishing—good people—who simply do not want to or cannot afford to start seeing differently. It may cost them their self-identity, or their job, or their perception of a press or an industry they love. When I started seeing differently, I had to leave, and I loved Seal Press like my own child. I had grown it, tended to it, and cared for it and was highly invested in my iden-tity as a Seal Press editor. So I understand that it's not an easy thing to ask people working in the traditional world to open up, to think differently, or to question the status quo.

And yet, many of us are doing just that. As is the case in most change movements, the initial subversive efforts come from those who know the system well. Change takes people working from the inside, with the right knowledge of the issues, skill sets, and capacity to articulate what's wrong. Subversion also requires that we be brave—that we speak out, that we refuse to be treated like second-class citizens, that we name things that don't feel fair. It's important that you become an independently published author or a publisher before you truly tackle advocacy issues, because you want to be taken seriously—as a change-maker, as an author, and/or as a publisher who's proven yourself. You need to have published a book well and to be so proud of that book that any attempts from the industry to qualify you or your book or press as "other" or "less-than" land with a solid *thud*. Newbies coming into publishing are looked upon a bit like a California hippie moving to the Deep South: there's a learning curve, and it takes some time, and a lot of trial and error, to get to the place where you'll be seen as "one of them," if you ever arrive there. And many authors simply don't have the aptitude, which we covered in Chapter 3, those authors who've self-published one book decide to look for other publishing partnerships. They did it once, and they don't want to deal with the frustrations and barriers that are a natural part of entering this industry as a self-published author. But authors and publishers who love this industry and are up to the challenge ahead of them must be prepared to hold their own and to be unflappable in a culture that is constantly undermining their efforts.

Convention Matters

Now that we've talked a bit about subversion and why that's what it's going to take to level the playing field, we must recap the value of "doing it right." I see myself as a bit of a rabble-rouser in the industry, writing about injustices and attempting to take the industry and big publishing to task, but when it comes to the books I publish, I care about nothing more than getting them as perfect as they can be.

I knew when I founded She Writes Press that we were going to need to work twice as hard, and have sound and consistent quality in our editorial and production, in order for the industry to take us seriously. All it takes is publishing one book outside the traditional paradigm to be smacked upside the head with the prevailing "us versus them" (traditional versus everyone else) mentality of the publishing industry. But for me, having been immersed in traditional publishing, and knowing what it felt like to be in the inner circle, the double standards I felt were more pronounced and stung a bit more.

Over the years, I've witnessed and heard directly from friends who have faced overt discrimination about the ways in which minorities desiring entry into certain industries have to be better than the best in order to have even a fighting chance—whether we're talking about medicine or law or engineering. If a person of color wants to rise to the top of their industry, they strive to be the best in a way their nonminority colleagues don't have to. Because of the dynamic in the publishing industry, this is the exact position indie authors find themselves in. There is no room for error. Substandard editorial quality, bad cover design, amateur interiors, and rookie mistakes are reasons for the industry to write you off. There will be no discussion about it, and no second chances. Errors and oversights simply prove that you don't know what you're doing, and there's little hesitation from reviewers, bookstore owners, librarians, and other industry movers and shakers to simply ignore you and any requests you might make on behalf of your book. To get your foot in the door with these people, you need to talk the talk, walk the walk, and have a book that is indistinguishable from—or better than—those of your traditional counterparts. You need to anticipate industry professionals' questions and be ready to hold your own in conversation with them. You want always to be ready to give away copies of your book when you make requests for engagements or for bookstores to carry it. And if an industry insider looks at your book and thinks it looks self-published, that's basically the end of the conversation—and they may or may not be direct enough to tell you why.

Independent authors and publishers, therefore, have a mandate: to do better than their traditional counterparts. They have to hire the right people and spare no expense. I've often argued that you cannot produce a book design that rivals that of a big house for $100 through 99Designs.com. You just can't. It might be good, or good enough, but to really stand out, you need to be pushing the envelope with your designs and staying on top of or ahead of the trends. If you're not a cover designer, don't try to be. Hire out—and this goes for everything you don't believe yourself to be an expert at doing.

Book publishing conventions are not up for debate. *The Chicago Manual of Style* should be your bible for editorial matters. You should have a house style or just default to *Chicago*. You need to find great editors, and book designers who are experts, who've designed books—not a friend's daughter who's a graphic designer who wants a shot at designing a book cover. Authors can and do often find good artwork for their covers, but they rarely, in my experience, have a sense of what makes a good composition. It takes years to cultivate a good eye for covers, and book design has conventions—like the hierarchy of the title, subtitle, and name, and attention to the way a book will look as a thumbnail on Amazon's and other online retailers' websites.

It bothers me that industry folks use the phrase "that looks self-published" to criticize a book's design, but I confess to doing it myself. "Self-published" has become a measure to qualify whether a book is worthy, so to be a self-published author and to have a book that does not look self-published is a compliment. It means that your book "passes," and that no reader or book buyer or librarian would be able to tell the difference between your book and a book coming out of one of the big houses. They are still the gold standard—no matter what we might think about some of their acquisitions choices. The big houses have rock-solid editorial and design processes, and while not every single book they publish deserves editorial and production awards, they're consistently good.

If and when indie authors surpass our traditional counterparts, that's great. But I have no qualms about saying that our goal is to be as good as they are, to have the same measures and expectations of quality. The big houses don't hesitate to spend good money on editorial and design. They don't cut corners. Yes, they make mistakes. I've seen traditionally published books with typos, editorial errors, incorrect running heads, and missing elements. But no one is shaming the big publishers for these errors. Perhaps this is a case of big publishers' having proven themselves and thus getting cut a little more slack. Perhaps they don't need to answer to their critics for their errors because of their legacy or because they've done it right so often. But I don't think so. If we look at why no one questions errors in books put out by big publishers through the lens of arguments I've been making in this chapter, their getting off the hook is about one thing: privilege.

As an indie author, you don't have that privilege. You may believe you've earned it. You may have put in equal effort and more money than your traditional counterparts, but that doesn't matter. This is not about what's fair. The only way indie authors can level the playing field is to actively strive for the same standards as, or better standards than, traditional publishers. We need to expect only the highest quality of ourselves and of one another, and hopefully someday the notion that something "looks self-published" will be a thing of the past.

What Makes a Book "Look" Self-Published?

While the old adage says "don't judge a book by its cover," the industry does judge books by their covers. When a book "looks" self-published, it's either missing something or doing something it's not supposed to be doing. This judgment is coming mostly from industry people, who are trained in looking at covers and catching errors. Many authors simply don't know what's bad about their cover. They don't know what they don't know. I've seen self-published authors go through a redesign process, and only with a side-by-side, before-and-after comparison can they admit that their original cover was not good.

I come across countless authors who want me to look at their self-published books, to assess them, and sometimes to consider republishing them on She Writes Press. It's not always the case that these books have poorly designed covers, but there are usually problems—with the image, the typography, the effects. Book covers have certain trends that come and go, and book designers follow these trends and stay up to date on what's happening in the industry in a way that authors, unless they're crazy cover enthusiasts, simply aren't doing. Many authors inadvertently create something that has an outdated vibe.

(continued on next page)

It's a lot like clothes. You might be drawn to what makes you comfortable. You might be stuck in the '80s, and that's cool. But if you were going to the Oscars, you would probably let someone else dress you, or at least choose something modern and flattering. Your book's debut is its Oscar night. It needs to look like it belongs alongside its competition—and if you're not sure what it takes to get it there, then you need to seek out support.

See the following section—"Top Ten Mistakes Newbie Authors Make, and How It Costs Them"—for specific examples of things that make a book look self-published, and make sure that your next book, whether it's your first or your fourth, is ready to rock its debut in style.

Top Ten Mistakes Newbie Authors Make, and How It Costs Them

A top-ten list with a negative slant can be a little shaming for authors if they see something on the list that they've done, but that's not my intention with this list. After all, some of these mistakes are ones I've made myself. You learn through trial and error, and people who've been in the industry and who've had a hand in creating many, many books can tell you about the mistakes that shaped their career. When you make a mistake in a final book, either the book lives with it forever or you spend a lot of money to destroy the books you've printed in order to correct the error. Both choices hurt. Some of the more memorable mistakes in books I've worked on include omitting the author biography; leaving off a bar code; inserting the wrong running heads. Early in my career, I approved a cover that had "Forward by" on the cover, rather than "Foreword by," and I have never mixed up the meanings of those two words since. At Seal Press, we had to destroy a print run of ten thousand books because the PMS color (we had opted for a two-color interior) in the interior of the book was wrong—a printing error, but still. Ouch.

It's hard to anticipate errors—sometimes they just happen. This is a creative business run by human beings. Sometimes it doesn't matter how many sets of eyes are on something. Errors get through. In the She Writes Press author handbook, we remind authors that errors will happen. Jack Shoemaker, a longtime publisher and legacy in the industry, says about errors that they let you know that books are made by humans, not gods. That said, a book with too many egregious errors just looks messy. So here we go:

1. BAD COVER DESIGN

Your cover is the first thing people look at, and it extends to the spine and the back cover. It's difficult to articulate what makes a cover work without showing images, but I do have a couple of She Writes Press redesigns to showcase here to give you a sense of a before-and-after. A professionally published book needs to have a logo on the spine and a clean back-cover design. I've seen books with professional-looking covers, only to turn the book around and see a formatting disaster. Don't try to shove too much text onto your back cover, and make sure your blurbs are formatted correctly—with em dashes in front of your endorsers' names, and proper credentials (e.g., "—Brooke Warner, publisher of She Writes Press and author of *What's Your Book?* and *Green-Light Your Book*").

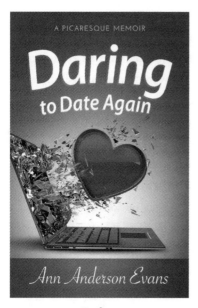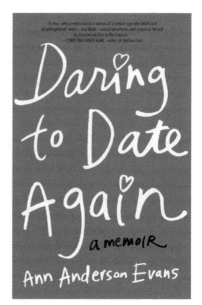

Before   After

2. BAD INTERIOR DESIGN

The tricky thing about interior design is that sometimes you don't know what it's going to look like until your book is in print. This happened to me with the first print run of my first book, *What's Your Book?* In a PDF file, it looked fine. Mine was the first book we published through She Writes Press, and it was another tough lesson when I opened that box of books and saw my interior. I considered destroying my own print run but ultimately didn't. The content was good, and the interior design wasn't horrible, but it wasn't to the standard of conventional publishing I was used to. Every book we've published since, by contrast, certainly has been, and I corrected my interior for a second print run. Sometimes your first books will take that hit, but it's worth it for what you learn.

Interior design has a lot of "best practices," including margin space, kerning (space between letters), and leading (space between lines). Certain fonts work better than others. I've been astounded by some of the assessments I've gotten back from trusted designers about things to fix in interior designs. Design is technical, and while there are plenty of programs out there that allow you to drop your book into a template, I wouldn't advise using those. Interior design is part of the artistry of book publishing. And while it's true that people might not notice anything off about a templated design, a beautiful interior will not be lost on them, either. Choices we might make in our book designs—whether it's to have deckled edges or spot gloss on the cover or a two-color interior—are things that help a book stand out in an industry where it's hard to rise above the noise.

3. PRICING

At a book reading I attended for an author acquaintance of mine, I was happy to buy the book at the end of the event, as I always am, to support the author and the bookstore. I handed over the book, and the cashier said, "That will be $28.14." What? The book was a slim paperback, and the author had priced it at $26.00, more expensive than most hardcovers I buy. I was in that situation where you feel like you're in too far to pull out, so I sucked it up and bought the book, but I felt ripped off. I understand why self-published authors do this. You've invested a lot of money in your book, and you want to make some of it back. But don't put it on your reader to make up your investment. Nothing smacks of self-published author more than a price point that's really off. Your book needs to be competitively priced. If you use the calculator at CreateSpace or IngramSpark and you see that you are not making enough of a margin on your book, then you might want to explore getting an offset print run. The economies of scale are such that you can get good pricing once you clear one thousand copies—though this is often too many books for most self-published authors to consider. Another final thing here is that this author was lucky to have gotten this bookstore reading, and it probably happened only because she knew the event coordinator or the owner. An overpriced book can also prevent a book from being carried in bookstores.

4. FAILING OR REFUSING TO GET A COPYEDIT OR A PROOFREAD

Next to the destruction of the huge print run at Seal I mentioned earlier, the second-saddest situation I witnessed involving destroyed books stemmed from an author's refusal to get a proofread. This was a flat-out error in judgment on her part. I guess she felt as if she'd already spent too much money on her book—for developmental editing and copyediting, and then for cover and interior design. She was looking to spend more money on marketing when it came out, so she skipped the proofread. (These three levels of editing—developmental, copyediting, and proofreading—are standard for all books. Some books won't get a developmental edit, because they don't need it, but every single title should get a copyedit, which is a line edit for grammar, punctuation, syntax, and repetition, and a proofread, which is a final pass for any final punctuation, spelling, or formatting errors that the copy editor might have missed.) This author was referred to me by a woman who'd endorsed her book with the caveat that she get the final version proofread. The author did not heed this advice, so, when the book came out, the endorser was rightfully angry and did not want her name associated with a manuscript that was full of errors she'd forewarned about. The author hired my team to do the proofread, and the result was glaring. The author was in tears and feared she'd self-sabotaged, but she wasn't even clear about *why*. She'd printed five hundred copies and decided to have them all destroyed. I supported this decision, but it was a costly and unfortunate mistake that was easily avoidable. No matter how many times your book has been edited, it needs a proofread. Don't skimp on editorial. It's not worth it.

5. FAILING TO FOLLOW PUBLISHING CONVENTIONS

You don't know what publishing conventions exist if you don't have previous industry experience, and moving ahead without regard for these conventions is one of the biggest giveaways of a self-published author. I've seen self-published authors do a lot of things in their books that could best be described as "cute," like using a silly author photo, fake blurbs, and too-clever cover copy. There's no editor or publisher there to curb the impulse to do so, so these authors make decisions that lead their book to "look self-published." Fake cover blurbs I've seen might be attributed to someone like, "Suzy Simple, best-selling author," when Suzy Simple does not exist. It's even worse if Suzy Simple is endorsing a book about how to simplify your life. The author is trying to be clever, but comes off looking amateur.

Less offensive, but still not following convention, is to list an Amazon review on the back cover of your book. This is bad form, and it can give away that you don't know what you're doing. Author biographies and photos should be überprofessional, even if your book is "cute." I've also read bios that are off-putting in their attempt to be clever. You have to remember that people don't know you, and what one person might find cute, another will find annoying. Keep your bio limited to what qualifies you to write the book you're writing and otherwise short, clean, and sophisticated. Some of the best-selling authors have the most to-the-point bios. In one of my favorite Seal Press memoirs, *Stranger Here,* author Jen Larsen's biography is simple and to the point: "Jen Larsen is a writer, editor, and proofreader living for less in Ogden, Utah. You can find her at jenlarsen.com." This is both short and relevant, and readers who are so inclined can discover more about her online.

6. MAKING YOUR BOOK NONRETURNABLE

Many new authors who've failed to do their homework about the publishing industry may be tempted to make their book nonreturnable. In doing so, you will not be able to sell your book into the trade, you will effectively cut off any possibility that bookstores or wholesalers will carry it, and, furthermore, you will mark yourself as a self-published author. In Chapter 6, I write about how problematic it is that book publishing is a returns-based industry, but this is yet another place where you want to work within the system to change the system. Making your book nonreturnable does not make you a visionary; it makes you sell fewer books.

7. SETTING THE WRONG DISCOUNT

This is the same as making your book nonreturnable, but with a different twist. Bookstores' expectation is that you will set your book's discount at 55 percent. You're given the option to do so when you set your book up with CreateSpace or IngramSpark. Anything less than 55 percent, and you prevent your book from being ordered by bookstores and wholesalers. If you don't care about selling to bookstores, you can choose a lower discount. Some authors might, for instance, set a 30 percent discount. This means that accounts have to pay 70 percent of your list price (as opposed to 45 percent with the standard discount). On the surface, this looks really good. Instead of getting paid $9 on a $20 book, you're getting paid $14. But this is all theoretical. Book sales are about volume, and you choke off any real capacity for distribution when you try to increase your own margins by trying to get other people (whether retailers or customers) to pay more than they're accustomed to paying for books. Should books be valued more? Yes. Is it an injustice that accounts pay you only 45 percent of your list price per book and that you're paid only a small portion of that once Ingram or Amazon or your publisher takes their fee? Yes. Is manipulating your pricing and discounting the best workaround to solve this problem and get more cash in your pocket? Absolutely not.

8. OMITTING METADATA THAT MATTERS

As I wrote in Chapter 6, most authors don't realize just how much metadata is associated with a single book title, so the likelihood that you're going to omit something is really high unless you're working with someone who knows about metadata and is going to guide you through the process and make sure you have everything in place. When you self-publish, very little metadata is required. The pieces that you must include when publishing on CreateSpace or IngramSpark are: cover image, trim size, price, description, author bio, keywords, and categories. These companies calculate the price points for foreign territories so you don't have to think about it, but that's it. They're not requiring your author bio or reviews/endorsements, which you want to be showcasing, especially if you have favorable reviews, to name the most important data that might get inadvertently omitted. You can add metadata to your title in a number of ways: through your publisher, if you have one, and through your individual platforms (like IngramSpark or CreateSpace, or digital-only platforms like Kindle, Nook, and Kobo). You can also add metadata through Author Central on Amazon. When you self-publish, it's hard to streamline your metadata, because you don't have a good, single point of entry. You're juggling many accounts (and many user names and passwords). If you're publishing prolifically, you might want to consider a service like Firebrand Technologies to help you have greater reach—and more accurate, streamlined data.

9. TRYING TO BE TOO OUTSIDE THE BOX

I want to preface this point by saying that sometimes it's good to think outside the box. In book publishing, outside-the-box thinking, however, is generally equated with not knowing what you're doing. So if you're going to try something, run it by some open-minded industry professionals to see what they think. This is the most uncreative creative industry you can imagine, and because a lot of people have been doing their thing for years and years, they meet any change with a raised eyebrow. Booksellers are notorious for not wanting things that "don't make sense," like books with unusual trim sizes or books with too many pages. They're picky about price points matching up with a book's perceived worth. They don't like books that come with "companion merchandise" unless it's very, very easy for them to sell. For instance, if you have a children's book that comes with a toy, you will need to either sell that toy to the store separately or make it a freebie. But there are lots of rules! And you do need to follow them, or you risk your product's simply not being carried.

On the digital front, outside-the-box thinking might include things like category flooding. I've seen authors choose nine categories for their book, instead of the usual two or three, but doing so actually dilutes the book's capacity to reach its markets, so it's not good outside-the-box thinking, though on the surface it might seem to be.

10. WRONG OR MISSING ELEMENTS

The most common error I see among self-published authors is a bar code that doesn't have the price embedded. This is a small issue, but it showcases right away to a bookstore owner that the book is both self-published and print-on-demand (see image). The four zeroes following the 9 effectively states that the book has no price, or that the price point is zero.

Other common missing elements might include a logo on a book's cover, a Library of Congress control number (LCCN) on the copyright page, and running heads in a book's interior. An author might just omit a logo because they're intending to publish only one book, and that's fine, but you never know if you'll be publishing more, and logos give a book's design an anchor and an added degree of sophistication. An LCCN is a number that gets assigned to a book from the Library of Congress, but you have to apply for it. Not knowing that you're supposed to is just another aspect of not knowing what you don't know, but it can stand out to those in the industry as an oversight or a mistake.

Running heads are those single lines, often at the top or bottom of a page, or running along the side of a page, that indicate the author's name, the title of the book, or the title of the chapter. It's amazingly common to see books without running heads, another publishing convention that, when overlooked or omitted, can point to a self-publishing mistake. I often see type running the wrong direction on a spine as well. Type should run downward, so that when you pick up a book and turn to look at the spine, the type runs left to right when the book is right side up. Failure to do this makes your spine stand out on a shelf because it will be the only book whose type runs the wrong way.

It's tough to be a visionary in this business, because you have to think through whether your creative idea is truly creative or whether it's something you think is interesting and unique but which might rub industry people the wrong way. You can test out your idea by getting expert opinions. Join an organization like the Independent Book Publishers Association or the Association of American Publishers. Talk to experts. Float your idea and see what people think, and take the feedback to heart. Be conscious of the fact that this industry has deep roots and does not take well to renegade ideas. It's a traditional industry with some ideas about things that very much need to be shaken up. But the things it does well should be emulated. Our job as indie authors, therefore, is to figure out how to be visionaries in this industry—how to shake things up, to level the playing field—while doing it in a way that proves we know exactly what we're doing.

The Difference Between a Visionary and a Renegade

In my first book, *What's Your Book?*, I wrote about the renegade author as a cautionary tale. We live in a culture that celebrates rebels and outlaws, so sometimes renegade authors fancy themselves change-makers operating outside the system and raising hell. There are two ways to raise hell, though—within the system or on the outskirts. And there are two energetic approaches to raising hell—one motivated by anger and the other motivated by desire for change. It's not to say those desiring change aren't ever propelled by anger (they are), but true visionaries have a higher purpose. We don't think of visionaries as people who are out of control or who do what they do on a whim. They have a vision and clarity, and if they're raising hell, they're doing so from a place of logic and within the system they're trying to disrupt. The most famous disrupters we all know are those who've effected change on a global level, those who've worked to fight against injustice and for equality—people like Martin Luther King, Jr., Nelson Mandela, Mother Teresa, Angela Davis, and Harvey Milk. These change-makers have fought for racial and social justice and gender equality. And while I don't believe that fighting for equality in the field of publishing is on par with the causes these leaders embraced, the parallels here are important. As indie authors working within the system to effect change, we need to harness the energy of leaders we admire and to remember that we make the greatest strides when we come from a place of humility and respect, even if and when we're upset by the injustices and inequalities we're witnessing.

The renegade author, by contrast, doesn't care to figure out why things are done the way they are done. They simply do what they want, with an attitude of *everyone else be damned*. The problem, of course, is that they damn themselves in the process. I've worked with authors who are so intent on their children's artwork being featured in their book that they don't care that the average reader will not find their child's artwork "special." Authors often want a personal element on their covers, to their own detriment. Memoir is an exception, because oftentimes the perfect image for a memoir is a family photo, but authors tend to choose things that look like snapshots, that date the book, and that in general don't have professional polish.

You might not see yourself as a renegade if you self-published and did everything yourself, but if you did not seek outside opinions from professionals who have experience in book publishing, then you inadvertently went a bit renegade. Authors who consciously choose not to get edited or not to get an outside professional opinion of their covers, or who do "cutesy" things like I mentioned above—putting a fake blurb on their back covers, or trying to be funny in their author biography—are being renegade. I often say that the value of the expert opinion is to help you uncover what you don't know. It is nearly impossible to get objective opinions from friends and family about your book.

To be a visionary and to work within the system, you want to be part of a larger community of publishers and authors, of people who know about your genre. You want to set up relationships with experts and have trusted advisors who will tell you if something doesn't look good. Self-published authors often want to save money, so they learn to do book design themselves. If I were to put a number on how often this is successful, I'd throw out 5 percent of the time. All over the Internet, you'll find people selling their inexpensive design services, but those designs are not going to help you achieve that gold standard we've been talking about throughout this chapter.

There is room for new ideas in book publishing, and trend-setters do break new ground in editorial, production, and design. You can be a visionary in these areas, but if you're stepping outside what's traditionally done, ask industry people for their thoughts about what you're doing. I would argue that the best place to be a visionary is in sales and marketing, which present endless opportunities for authors to rise above their competition. It requires that you be tireless in your efforts, but some of the most creative ideas I've seen from authors these days have happened in their postpublication efforts. For example, Jeff Goins, author of *The Art of Work*, launched a major campaign to give away thousands of copies of this book. All the reader had to do was pay shipping and handling—$6 or so. In exchange, Goins got e-mail addresses galore and the reader entered into a very well-executed drip-marketing campaign that featured videos of Goins upselling his audience. Smart.

Pins and memes are another visionary tool people are using to get word out about their books. These are designed jpegs that might feature quotes from you or images that speak to your audience. Social media is supervisual, and there's nothing more shareable than images, so this is a way to increase shares and likes and follows. Elizabeth Gilbert regularly features inspiring pins that get shared like crazy online, so check out her Facebook page if you're looking for a good example of how to do this right.

Spend your efforts on figuring out what works. Emulating others can be a first step toward becoming a visionary, because you are testing the waters and figuring out what's successful about what others are doing. To be a visionary, you need to spend some money. A lot of people are giving their books away by the truckload. Andy Sernovitz, author of *Word of Mouth Marketing*, told the audience at his Pub U panel that I attended in 2015 that he'd printed ten thousand galleys of his book to give away. At that quantity, his galleys were probably about 80 cents a pop. Still, that's not chump change. He spent eight grand on his galleys alone. But do you think he flooded the marketplace?

Yes. Do you think he got noticed? I know he did. People like Goins and Sernovitz might have a visionary strategy because their goals are about increasing their following over selling lots of copies of their book. They're willing to give their books away to get the following, with the idea of capturing people's e-mail addresses (and their attention) to sell them more stuff in the future. In business school, this is called a "funnel," where you capture people at a $0–10 price point and then cultivate the relationship to upsell bigger-ticket items—like classes, consulting packages, etc.—down the road.

Consider your tendencies. If you tend to buck against authority, remember that the industry is not the authority here. Your reader is. But your reader has been groomed from a lifetime of reading traditionally published books to have certain expectations—about the touch, the design, the price point of a book. They might not be able to consciously articulate what they like about a book, but what they like is all the things that set apart the professionals from the rookies. Remember what I said at the outset of this chapter: there is no room for error. Substandard editorial quality, bad cover design, amateur interiors, and rookie mistakes are reasons for the industry to write you off. Work within the system. Spend your money and efforts on getting it right the first time and every subsequent time. Don't be fueled by anger; be fueled by desire.

Chapter 8.

Discoverability

If you read about publishing, you're likely to have heard about the problem authors and publishers face with discoverability. In a nutshell, discoverability is the process by which an author's intended readers find his or her book. Discoverability is tough to achieve because there's so much out there competing for readers' attention, and publishers are desperate to come up with solutions to the discoverability problem. The fact that discoverability even is a problem may give us pause, since the rise of independent publishing is part of the reason there are so many books in the marketplace. While some traditional publishers may blame self-publishing for their loss of a stronghold in the marketplace, I say we all start on even ground. It's a fact that the sheer abundance of titles poses a challenge, but it's not insurmountable.

The discoverability problem exists in theory for any author long before they're even thinking about publishing a book, but the time you'll likely start to think about it is once you're published and your focus turns from writing and preparing to spreading the word about your book. Your goal is singular: to get your book in front of potential readers. But even if a reader does find your book, the challenge for you as an author continues. They have to buy it and read it, and for your book to catch on, they have to give it good reviews, talk about it, and share it. Word of mouth is not the only way a book skyrockets into people's awareness these days, but it certainly moves books. And, as we discussed in Chapter 3, due to social media, word of mouth has an even more reverberatory effect than it used to.

In 2015, I went on a family vacation to the Pacific Northwest. We stopped at a small shoe store in an artsy little town a couple hours outside of Seattle. There on the counter was a stack of novels with a placard on top that said WRITTEN BY A LOCAL AUTHOR. Part of me thought this was cool, but the cynical part of me wondered whether anyone was buying these books. Yet this was undoubtedly a small effort toward discoverability. Placing your books on the counter at a store might be one touch point. If a potential buyer later saw your book reviewed, maybe they'd be motivated to buy.

In 2014, Oprah Winfrey mounted an eight-city tour that her agent told me was conceived directly around discoverability. Her speakers were all authors of multiple books. Oprah sold her own books and the speakers' books and other "Oprah picks"—no doubt by the thousands—at giant pop-up bookstores. There are few people in this world who can successfully devise a tour focused on inspiring people to buy tons of books, but that's Oprah for you.

There are multiple pathways to discoverability, most of which require a lot of diligent effort on your part. Some of the things you can do that are geared toward discoverability include discounting, giveaways, social media interactions, getting reviews, advertising, and harnessing the power of your personality. There's a tapestry of choices, and authors need to be deliberate and conscientious in their approach. This chapter goes somewhat hand in hand with Chapter 9, in which we'll focus on community and connection, because one way to get discovered is to engage your community and to focus on cultivating and growing your readership, which involves keeping them interested and engaged. So while discoverability is a real challenge all authors face, the more you understand what you can do about it, the more confident you'll feel that you're not swimming in a riptide but rather making real headway toward your goal of gaining visibility for your book.

Five Shades of Book Discoverability

Andrew Rhomberg, founder of Jellybooks, has written about what he calls the "five shades of book discovery" that stimulate readers to discover books. This list was previously published by Writer's Digest *and is reprinted here with permission.*

1. Serendipitous Discovery: This is stumbling over a book either randomly or in a semidirected fashion that was not based on a Google-esque search, where we already knew the title or author of what we were looking for. This is what browsing a bookshop or a library shelf is all about.

(continued on next page)

2. Social Discovery: This is good ole word of mouth. Books that trusted friends recommend to us (and we might trust their recommendations only in certain subjects or genres where we think they have authority) and what is also happening on Goodreads, Readmill, Pinterest, Twitter, Facebook, Tumblr, and other social online destinations. We try a book or buy it because somebody else recommended it specifically to us or in a broadcasted recommendation to their friends and followers.

3. Distributed Discovery: We make many book discoveries when a book is mentioned in context, be it the review section of a newspaper, on a blog, at a conference, as a footnote or endnote in another book, etc. Increasingly we find links to Amazon and Goodreads attached, and soon we may see more sophisticated ways in which authors and publishers will embed book discovery into such situations.

4. Data-Driven Discovery: This is the Last.fm of book discovery, or the Netflix recommendation engine for movies applied to books. This might be an iPad or web app that learns from our past reading list (and what our friends are reading or recommending to us) to suggest new reads, but is more likely to be embedded into a retail shop front or a reading app. This can be as blunt as Amazon's recommendation system or a subtle personalization system that surfaces some books into our viewing range in preference over others without our even noticing (a very subtle form of hand selling).

5. Incentivized Discovery: Be it a promotion, book giveaway, or review copy, incentivized discovery has been with us for a long time. Readers can be tempted by the free or the great bargain. Increasingly we will see new data-driven, social, or personalized models for creating incentivized discovery.

Discounting

This discussion about discounting pertains only to e-books because e-books are the only product over which you have pricing control as an author. Discounting is a tricky topic because, on the one hand, I believe that too heavily discounting your book devalues your work, while on the other, doing so is a legitimately good discoverability tool. But that's book publishing for you—paradoxes abound.

The reason e-book discounting is so successful as a means of discoverability is that an entire subindustry has sprung up around getting word out about discounted e-books. When the idea to start pricing e-books at 99 cents first started, authors were regularly seeing spikes in their print sales, and even in their e-book sales after they returned to their original list price. But those days of consumers buying full-cost print and e-books as a result of a discounting campaign have passed, in part because discounting is now so flipping common.

If you look at the sidebar on pages 207–209, discounting falls into both data-driven and social discovery. Many She Writes Press authors have discounted their books through BookBub, a company/website (known also for being choosy) that features discounted books and that, because of its popularity, generally results in tons of downloads and authors' books shooting up in their Amazon rankings. You used to be able to launch a discounting campaign without the help of a service like BookBub, but if you want to see the kind of numbers BookBub campaigns seem to deliver on a regular basis—downloads in the tens of thousands—you have to partner with a company like this that has the eyes of hundreds of thousands of readers as a result of its very large database.

For most authors, the allure of discounting their e-book is strong. There are a lot of pros: reaching a new or different audience; having reason to talk up your book again; experiencing the adrenaline rush of watching your Amazon ranking soar. And there's the possibility of hitting best-seller lists, another huge pro I hadn't considered until fall 2015 when She Writes Press author Lene Fogelberg, author of the memoir *Beautiful Affliction*, hit the *Wall Street Journal* best-seller list as a result of the spectacular results of her BookBub campaign. However, the cons are definitely there, and the devaluation of your book that I mentioned at the outset of this section is the strongest one. Amazon has in effect trained people to expect a very low price on their e-books. Amazon's self-publishing e-book platform, Kindle Direct Publishing, forces authors to price their books between $2.99 and $9.99 if the author wants to keep 70 percent of their profits. If you price outside those parameters (meaning below $2.99 or above $9.99), then Amazon keeps 70 percent for itself and gives the author just 30 percent. This arrangement, combined with the popularity of discounting campaigns, has created a culture of free (or next-to-free) books, which does nothing but make us, collectively, value books less. When I wrote a blog post on this topic, arguing for parity pricing for e-books (meaning pricing e-books the same as paperbacks), people went through the roof in their comments, writing that parity pricing was a delusional strategy on the part of publishers. That readers expect lower price points for their ebooks has now been corroborated, in fact, by the release of Author Earnings' September 2015 report, which delivered some important tidbits of information, including:

- So far in 2015, the AAP's reports had charted a progressive decline in both e-book sales and overall revenue for the AAP's member publishers; and
- during that same period in 2015, Amazon's overall e-book sales had continued to grow in both unit and dollar terms, fueled by a strong shift in consumer e-book purchasing behavior away from traditionally published e-books and toward indie-published and Amazon imprint–published e-books.

Nevertheless, my point stands: discounting mania is not good for authors. That said, when the time comes for you to consider a discounting campaign, for all the alluring reasons I mentioned above, please wait until your book has been out a good four to six months, if not a year. Books are like movies, in that you blink and a just-released movie is available on cable. Both industries are fast-driving and reactive. If a movie doesn't go gangbusters in its first few weeks, it's out of the theaters, and the same is true in book publishing. Wait a couple weeks, and the book you're considering buying for $9.99 will be on sale for 99 cents. But instead of being driven by the studios, book discounting is generally driven by authors themselves.

Good times to move forward on discounting your books

are tie-in dates—for instance, Mother's Day; New Year, New You; Earth Day; Teacher Appreciation Day. When you discount, make sure you're working with an expert or a company like BookBub. Doing it on your own is a waste of time. Most authors I talk to after their fire sales feel anywhere from ambivalent to content about their campaigns. They're happy they got so many downloads, and they feel a little empty about having sold so many books for so little profit. As with a garage sale when you're selling something you feel a bit ambivalent about selling and then someone comes along and tries to haggle for it for cents, it's not a fair-market exchange, and both parties know it.

As long as you're aware of this going in, it's okay. I say focus on the bigger goal of using the opportunity to talk up your book to your existing audience, who may or may not have bought your book in the first place. And if you get thousands of downloads at 99 cents, you will have earned a bit of pocket change, and most people aren't going to begrudge that. That said, I'd love to see us all push back against discounting mania and let books sell for the already-low retail cost most of them bear.

Branding

Many new (and even some established) writers balk at the idea of themselves as a brand, and yet they are, and should be working toward becoming one before their first book is published—even if only on a small scale. Branding is related to discoverability in that your choice of logo, color, images, and aesthetic carries across your website, your printed materials, and your social media. If you have something recognizable and consistent that people see a few times, they will recognize you and remember you. This is how discoverability begins—being enough of a voice rising above the crowd that people want to come back for more.

For a lot of people thinking about branding, a particular "look" comes to mind. Branding is about your logo and your collateral materials and your colors, yes, but it's also about cohesiveness. This means that your social media platforms should all have the same look. They should showcase your author photo (or at least an avatar), rather than an image of a sunset or a group photo. Your banner should be the same across all social media, and as soon as you have a book cover, you can create (or have created for you) a banner that features your book cover, along with its release date.

Branding yourself as an author goes beyond social media and into your website and the content you put out into the world. Content falls into the data-driven category of discoverability because anytime you publish anything, you want to include your book (along with a corresponding hyperlink to the retailer of your choice, if possible) in your byline. As soon as your book is available to preorder, update your biography anywhere it might be live to include this hyperlink. The more you publish, the more your bio shows up in the world, and if it consistently features your book, you will gain some traction, especially if you keep up your online publishing efforts through guest posts and free and for-pay published articles alike. It's all about exposure.

That you will continue to push content speaks to the fact that the destination of your journey as author does not end with publishing your book. The job of branding yourself lasts forever, as long as you intend to keep publishing. I should be able to land on an author's website and see a commonality between their site and their social media. And you, the author, provide the continuity. The book is simply one product, hopefully of many, that you will create to enhance your brand over the course of your career as an author. This is why you always want to create an author site and author-based social media over a book site or book-based social media. In almost every case, you will outlast your book's popularity.

The branding of you reaches into another form of discoverability beyond social, which is incentivized discoverability. When you have a website and social media, you can do your own promotions, give away your book, and create campaigns to engage your readership—driving up your number of likes and followers, but also driving sales. When you do promotions for your book, the number-one thing you want to be focused on is capturing people's e-mail addresses, since as we discussed in Chapter 3, e-mail addresses are gold, much more important than numbers of social media followers, because these are the readers you can market to directly.

You can build your database by running a promotion, like giving away copies of your book, but you might want to think bigger than that. Might you do a podcast leading up to your book's publication and give away copies of the book to people who sign up for your newsletter? Might you give away something that ties in to your book? Bloggers are famous for sweepstakes-style giveaways, and I've seen authors (some of whom are bloggers, of course) do this effectively as well. If the protagonist of your novel is a musician, maybe you give away four $50 iTunes cards, for instance. If you're writing a memoir that involves a difficult subject—alcoholism, abuse, addiction—maybe you give away a gift basket that includes a journal and a copy of your book, or offer to give a $100 donation to an organization that supports education or awareness surrounding the issue you write about. The possibilities here are endless, but the point is that people are crazy for giveaways—and when you have a new book out, there's a lot you can do to drive people to your site and to actively drive discoverability.

If you already have a website and social media and are already churning out ideas for your supercool giveaway, that's great, but do yourself a service before you launch your campaign, and get your online presence evaluated by a professional. This means calling up someone whose design work you admire and asking them for an evaluation of your site's aesthetics. You might have to cast your net to ask for recommendations for web designers, but there are countless companies doing beautiful design work. One way to find companies like this is to scroll down to the far-bottom-right corner of a site you admire and see whether a design company's name appears there. You can typically click through these links and find information about the company that designed the site.

Because I work with authors on their platforms, I'm often astounded by the 1990s websites people have and the mishmash that's happening across their social media. Part of having a strong author presence is having attractive, polished "assets." Your assets are your book cover, your social media banners, your author photo, and anything else your audience is taking in visually. Your website also has to be functional enough to be able to support a campaign like this, meaning that you have to have an e-mail marketing system—like MailChimp or Constant Contact—in place and functioning seamlessly. Before you do a giveaway, set up what's called a "bribe to subscribe" and give away something that's actually valuable, like a cool listicle (e.g., "10 Tips on Something You're an Expert On"), an audio series, or a drip campaign, which is a series of articles that are released at intervals so they end up in people's inboxes over the course of a few weeks. The possibilities are endless and limited only by the confines of your imagination. The more you can do something interesting and new and cutting-edge, the more likely you are to attract people's curiosity about and interest in what you're doing. The sky's the limit. Go forth, brand well, and get discovered.

Social Media

In Chapter 3, I broke down the components of platform and gave social media only 10 percent of the platform pie. As a discoverability tool, social media is given more credit than it's due, partly because too many authors start their social media when they decide they're going to publish their book. Unless it's going to take you several years to get published, it's simply too late in the game for your social media to become a valuable asset before your book comes out. I tell you this not so much to discourage you as to remind you that social media is just one discoverability tool you have, and not the most important one, especially in the beginning. Your primary focus with your social media should be to engage your potential readers. You do this by giving them information, sharing ideas, and prompting conversation by posing questions, but also with follow-backs, shout-outs, and retweets. Social media has a distinct you-scratch-my-back-I'll-scratch-yours flavor to it, so your following is and will be based largely on your generosity.

The most effective use of your social media is through giving. Ultimately you can and will promote your book, but in order to promote well, you must first give. I see new authors with brand-new social media presences blowing up the social stratosphere with self-promotion—starting with asks for follows and crowdfunding support and lasting all the way through publication. *Follow me! Support me! Buy my book!* These asks are not inappropriate in themselves, but don't be surprised if someone pulls a Janet Jackson on you in the form of *What have you done for me lately?* Get ahead of this response, rather than risking alienating your would-be fans, by giving. And I don't mean you should give stuff at this point—just good content. People should land on your social media pages and see that the majority of what you're posting is in the form of ideas and things you're interested in. Only about 10 percent should be self-promotional. Any more than that, and you will fatigue your readers or, worse, lose them.

Social media is social discovery, according to Rhomberg's five shades of book discovery—but note the last sentence about social discovery: "We try a book or buy it because somebody else recommended it specifically to us or in a broadcasted recommendation to their friends and followers." It's more often the case that readers will buy a book because someone else recommends it, and not because the author herself is peddling. So keep up the promoting of others as a priority, remember that what goes around comes around, and be patient.

Social media has a lot of potential for discoverability when it's used as a tool to engage, to post interesting stuff, and to give love to readers. (Elizabeth Gilbert is an amazing example of what an author love-fest looks like; if you don't already follow her, check out her Facebook page.) These authors are conscientious about promotion and, in turn, about their impact on their followers. They're using social media not to sell stuff but rather to create community and to enhance their presence and their brand. Consider, too, that the way you gain followers on social media is through shares. When people share your posts, they're saying to their friends and communities, *This is worth looking at.* If you're lucky, new people find you. This is discoverability in action. If the first thing a new convert sees is self-promotion, followed by another self-promotion piece and then another, you've probably already lost them.

In every new space, there are always going to be companies looking to find new ways to enhance a given experience, and there are many social media tools directed at authors. I want to mention Bublish here as one such example. Bublish considers itself a social platform that allows authors and readers to interact by providing a means for authors to upload excerpts and new content—like author bio info, little-known facts, behind-the-scenes stories—that readers might be interested in. The site's goal is to create a more intimate and direct experience of books and their authors—and to increase discoverability and therefore sales.

The main problem I see with these tools has to do with author bandwidth. There are tons of cool new things out there for authors to do, but it's difficult to juggle the primary social media sites, let alone new sites that require a whole new level of attention and tending. That said, if you have unlimited capacity for new tools, you'll find all kinds of fun things to explore. Type in "social media book discovery tools" on Google, and explore to your heart's content.

No matter what social platforms you engage on, keep in the forefront of your mind whether a post might be share-worthy.

What do you like, favorite, retweet, and share—and why? If you have something you think has share potential, promote it for $5, $10, or $20 to increase its visibility. Spending a little money— like $20 a month—on social media advertising is a worthwhile expense if you're focused on building a following.

When your book comes out, limit your self-promoting posts to one or two a week. You do not need to be sharing a blow-by-blow of your book tour or the results of a discounting campaign or posting every single review you get to social media. You just don't. Even if you're excited about these things, your audience will tire easily of this kind of coverage. You can easily do a single round-up of your best reviews in one post by listing them on a page on your website and posting once you're excited about the good reviews you're receiving, along with a link to that page on your site. Be strategic and discerning, and remember that since social media will never hold a candle to your database, you might want to use your valuable promotional posts to drive people to your site—through giveaways, downloads, or even an occasional media round-up.

Ultimately, be careful not to be that parent who has eyes only for their own baby and never acknowledges anyone else's. Keep all of these best practices in mind, and your social media will be a solid discoverability tool that will give your book an occasional boost.

Reviews

Reviews fall under distributed discovery, meaning that your book is getting notice because it's being referred to in a speech;

written about in a magazine, newspaper, or journal; or referenced in an online publication or book. You typically can't influence other decision-makers to refer to or write about your book, but you can actively work toward reviews. Trade reviews are all-important for novels and memoirs, though not unimportant for other kinds of books; it's just that they can mean the difference between a breakout and a dud when it comes to fiction and memoir. Industry people, for one, read reviews. And if your book shows up across multiple review outlets, readers of said reviews—people like librarians, book buyers, and even editors—will take notice.

The five most important trade review outlets, as of the writing of this book, are *Publishers Weekly, Kirkus, Booklist, Library Journal,* and *Shelf Awareness.* Of these, *Publishers Weekly* and *Kirkus* have self-publishing-specific review guidelines, where you pay to get reviewed. In my experience, it doesn't particularly matter whether you get a traditional or paid review; as long as you get a good review from one of these sites, it carries some weight—people sit up and take notice. If you qualify to submit traditionally to these outlets, always try this method first. If you don't get assigned a review, you might want to consider paying. It's not right for everyone, and not necessarily the best use of your publicity campaign dollars, but, again, it matters for some genres more than for others, and a strong review from one of these outlets might end up opening doors and can certainly increase the likelihood of your book's getting into libraries. Librarians read trade reviews, and they often base their buys on what they're seeing in the pages of these industry magazines.

Online reviews are also important for visibility. I've heard that fifty reviews is the magic number Amazon is looking for to give you a little extra attention. You need Amazon reviews in order to launch a discounting campaign, because reviews speak to buyers and showcase what people think about your book. Amazon reviews have gotten a little contentious, as Amazon's review policy has intensified and now bars authors from reviewing people they know or people perceived to be their friends. This kind of review policing happens because reviews may seem to present a conflict of interest. My advice to people who are writing Amazon reviews is to admit that they know the author, or that they got a free copy of the book in exchange for a fair review. Amazon may still prohibit these reviews from going live, but I've seen reviews like this on Amazon, and my sense is that reviewers who name the truth of the situation are more likely to see their reviews go through.

Lots of companies are trying to capitalize on this kind of discovery by allowing readers to post directly from their sites (or from connected apps) about books they're reading and liking. One such service is Aerbook, which is thinking creatively about distributed discovery. Ron Martinez, founder of Aerbook, told *Publishers Weekly* that his platform is a form of "native commerce that produces interactive social content and links to purchasing opportunities that can be sent down the social streams of targeted consumers, alongside their posts, RTs, and social chitchat." Aerbook is finding ways to push book content out to online social media platforms, and, by including links to buy, it's offering a new form of distribution. If an author is the only one pushing out their own content, chances are, their followers will tolerate that only to a point. But if Aerbook is used in the way it's intended, it functions as a review system, allowing readers to share excerpts or just to post on social media with a link to the book, which includes buy buttons.

My parting advice is simply to take reviews seriously. Ask people who've read your book to review it online. Build up your Goodreads community and review other people's work—without the expectation of a return review. But if the author you're reviewing is a colleague who's writing in your genre or on a similar topic, you might get to know them on the Interwebs, and there might come a point when they return the favor.

Send your book out for review—not only to the trades, but broadly. Independent authors might have a hard time getting noticed by major news outlets, but you never know. Some papers have discriminatory policies against indie authors, but not all of them. You want to cast your net wide and consider both broad and niche readerships. If you have the resources to hire a publicist, brainstorm with them about review possibilities explicitly, and see what you can gather up in support of your book. It helps with discoverability, each new review serving the purpose of lighting up the marquee that is your book until it shines brightly and people start to say, "Hey, yeah, I've heard about that book."

Advertising

To advertise or not to advertise? What impact does it really have, and will it result in sales? The truth is that the results of advertising are incredibly difficult to measure. When you pay for ads, the outlet you're paying will be able to tell you only what their circulation is, or how many page clicks their site gets on average.

They likely won't have or won't share stats on how their advertisements affect book sales. That said, any industry magazine that you pay to advertise appreciates your business so much that they're likely to continue to give you accolades as a result of your good business. I've seen this play out many times, actually.

Consider this tale of two authors. Two different authors—Author A and Author B—are reviewed in an industry magazine. The magazine reaches out to both of them and asks if they want to advertise in the next issue. Author A says yes. She secures an ad to the tune of $500 or $1,000. Author B says no, I don't think it's worth it. Two months later, Author A gets an e-mail from the magazine letting her know that they've selected her in their round-up of best books of the year in her category, and asking whether she wants to advertise again. Author B does not receive a follow-up e-mail.

Does this smack of industry nepotism? Yes, but this is how it works. Magazines need funding to survive. Advertising is a primary revenue generator. Authors who pay to advertise get their backs scratched, and I've seen evidence that the more they advertise, the more opportunities they get. I've seen authors advertise a few times in a particular industry magazine and later get a full-page author feature. These aren't flukes.

Publishers have known for years that you have to pay to play. It's part of the reason big publishers get their books reviewed and featured more than small presses or individual authors. Magazines and journals go back to the well of the publishers with deep pockets. They rely on them to meet their quotas. There's a give and a take, and both parties understand this, regardless of whether they're willing to acknowledge the inherent favoritism at play. This kind of discovery falls somewhere among and between social and data-driven discovery. It should probably have a category all its own, because it's a legitimate use of authors' campaign dollars, and discoverability through advertising is one of its known benefits. The hard part about advertising is that its results are hard to measure and quantify, but I encourage you to experiment. I mentioned spending $20 a month on social media advertising; this is just one small way in which you can experiment, and if your book gets a review in an industry magazine or wins an award, consider your advertising options carefully. It might be worth it for the long-term gains.

Your Personality and Engagement

This is the most creatively challenging of the discoverability tools, and one that Rhomberg doesn't include in his list of five shades of book discovery, perhaps because it's not measurable, and perhaps because it's embedded to some degree in the social and the incentivized discovery. But I think it's a category all its own because author charisma, creativity, and drive lend a lot to discoverability. Authors who have the right personality for their particular area of expertise, or who engage with their community in such a way that the community rallies around them, succeed almost despite themselves. Authors who have major followings have a je-ne-sais-quoi quality that is usually not just about their books. It's about their capacity to spread the right message to the right group of people at the right time.

Some writers set out to create this kind of scenario. You can create a movement, as we'll discuss a bit more in Chapter 9. But creating a movement requires you to drill down into who your readership is and what makes them tick, and my sense is that truly successful authors more often than not stumble into their capacity as leaders of movements, rather than setting out to create them. Consider Susan Cain, who by all measures has created a movement among the introverts of the world with her best-selling *Quiet: The Power of Introverts in a World That Can't Stop Talking*. It's possible that Cain set out to create a movement, but more likely than not, she just got really excited and locked into an idea that was ripe for exploring, and then connected in a profound way with her readers, most of whom were introverts longing to be recognized and celebrated, which was the purpose of Cain's book. She now has a bit of a cult of celebrity, though I don't think that Cain has necessarily always been a supercharismatic person. But she's become charismatic as a result of her leadership and because she's taken on the mantle of a cause that so many people care about.

Other authors may start out with charisma. They might be natural go-to people whom others rally around. Jill Smokler, the founder of ScaryMommy.com, author of *Confessions of a Scary Mommy*, and arguably one of the most popular mom bloggers around, is ridiculously charismatic. She's cute, she's got attitude, she has a cute family, and she's not an egomaniac. Her site's tagline is "A parenting website for imperfect parents." She's tapped into something huge here—which is that all parents are imperfect, and they are sick of being told all the ways in which they could and should be better parents. So here's a woman who celebrates parental imperfection and showcases herself as the ultimate imperfect parent—the scary mommy. Totally brilliant.

Whether you think you have the kind of personality that can drive discoverability or not, don't worry about it too much in the beginning. You need to be who you are and not try to emulate or copy anyone else. Figure out what your unique offering is. Dig deep into your content and pull out the thing that most inspires you. Practice engaging on that topic. See if you can come up with some giveaways or simple content around that topic. Bring it up from your heart and see if you can start a conversation. It takes a while to get there, but you will start to feel a pulse around engagement. You will start to see what resonates and what falls flat, but the only way to experience this is to keep making an effort and to keep the conversation going—until you have a bigger personal platform, bigger engagement opportunities, and a bigger fan base. It will happen, but you must put your personality into the equation. Your eventual fans are looking for a person to connect with—someone underneath the writing. So if you want to be a successful author in today's publishing climate, and to have a real shot at discoverability, you must bring your whole self to the party. Let yourself be seen. Let your personality loose. It doesn't matter if you're reserved or wild—we're all drawn to different types of people for different reasons. You just have to be authentically you and then keep showing up, even on days and weeks when you don't feel like it. Be there for your readers, and they'll be there for you.

Chapter 9.

Community and Connection

One of the great ironies for writers, many of whom come to their craft for their love of solitude, for its inherent celebration of the introvert, is the degree to which being a modern author requires you to be out in the world. Becoming an author in today's culture means giving a face to your voice. There's an expectation, no matter how you publish, that if you can, you will: 1) promote; 2) pull in favors; 3) be visible online; 4) engage others. Part of your success as a writer lies in your capacity to community-build or to create connection. All successful writers do one or the other. And while some do so effortlessly, there are plenty of authors for whom this constant expectation to engage feels difficult, even burdensome. Which is why it's important for any author to find the ways in which they enjoy engaging and then dig deep there, rather than trying to force something they find tedious or even odious.

It's pretty amazing that to achieve any or all of the four expectations in the list above, you don't actually have to leave home. Introverted writer types can and do engage like gang-busters from their keyboards, in the comfort of their living room or home office. The level of enjoyment you derive from your activities online is going to depend a whole lot on the authenticity of the connections you make, and on your real availability and responsiveness to your community. Some writers may need to put parameters on how available they can be or want to be, for the simple reason that engaging online can turn into a full-time job, and most of us already have a nine-to-five job, in addition to trying to write on the side. But if you're not engaging at all—if you're a lurker who prefers never to comment on posts you read, if you resist talking about what you're doing on social media, if you resist social media altogether, if you never give shout-outs to other writers, if you don't retweet and like other people's posts—then you must take baby steps and start somewhere. Your availability to and engagement with the community you are working to either participate in or build is part of your success as an author, and your generosity of spirit is the key to connection.

I wrote in my last book how Kamy Wicoff, my cofounder at She Writes Press, has said that generosity is the new currency. This concept has stayed with me all these years and matters enough to now make its way into another book. It's something writers who are not naturally generous need to remember and try to cultivate. Generosity online comes in the form of celebrating others' successes, sharing or retweeting other people's posts, congratulating others on a job well done (like getting published). It also might manifest itself as good content that you provide—sometimes for free—to people who read your work, in the form of blog posts, guest posts, content giveaways on your website, and social media posts.

Your responses to people's comments to your work are also generosity in action. It takes time to acknowledge that people are responding to you, and it's one of the keys to good community building. Social media is an amazing connector, allowing us access to people we would never have been able to approach or be involved with in the past—whether because of distance or because of the degree of celebrity to which we might be removed from certain folks. Now, we can be in dialogue with other writers (writers we read and admire, as well as those we're in the trenches with) about topics we're passionate about. The dialogue part is important here. If it's a one-way conversation, that becomes quickly apparent, and you might lose some people if this is your preferred style.

There are many ways to be in community, and it's important that you give new ideas a chance, even if you're convinced that a certain way of engaging is not for you. I'm going to ask you to challenge yourself if you have preconceived notions about what community and connection mean to you. I work with so many authors who discount the power of online community, whose fixed frame about what community *should* mean comes from a pre-Internet context that they wear like a badge of honor. This approach does not get authors where they want to be. So consider where you are on this topic. Maybe you love engaging with your audience so much that it detracts from your writing; maybe you need a bit of reframing to wrap your mind around what you are willing to do to open up to the possibility that you might actually enjoy some of what you're being asked to do; maybe you want to understand how to best engage so that you can create those meaningful connections. In my experience, no matter what a writer is doing in any given moment to engage their community, they can always learn more. Note that I didn't say "do more"; indeed, some writers need to do less. But staying open to ideas, to new technologies and trends, and to different methods of engagement will ensure that you're always doing a handful of things that you really enjoy—and that's the key to maintaining a community, the foundation of your fan base.

Connection in the Twenty-First Century

I hear a lot of talk from writers about how people crave "real" connection. The person saying these words invariably believes that "real" means "in person" and, implicitly, that online connection is less-than. Your feelings (and possibly judgments) about online community are important to explore as you think about your future as an author. Some writers I work with accept their fate, putting up social media profiles because they think they have to. They tend to them in the most minimal ways after that, posting once every few months, which is the same as being inactive. Others outsource their social media, which is better than letting it wither on the vine; however, it shouldn't be surprising that these folks have not experienced the power of true connection online. They're not engaging online, and to feel connected, you must engage.

I have a handful of close friends who so hate Facebook that they boycott it like angry teenagers. They insist that Facebook breeds a culture of disconnect. They take issue with the word "friending." The fact that anyone would have thousands of online "friends" incenses them. They're very literal people, and their literalism blinds them to the fact that friendship can mean different things to different people, and that community has many permutations.

I remember a conversation over dinner in San Francisco with a successful author I worked with at Seal Press. Twitter was new, and I wasn't on it. I was complaining about it, using words I've since heard my own authors say: *It's so limiting. How can you possibly keep up? How can you have a real conversation with someone in 140 characters?* She looked at me and said, "You really don't get Twitter, do you?"

No, I didn't. I wasn't on the platform, and I was resisting it. And I was rationalizing my own decision by making Twitter stupid. But Twitter is not stupid, and in retrospect I wish I'd been a much earlier adapter than I was. But it took me a while to shift my own internal narrative about whether Twitter was a place where I felt like I could experience meaningful connections. It turns out, it is. I've fully changed my tune, but it took being willing to look at my resistance, see that it was there, and then admit that I was wrong, or at least being a little surly about the whole thing.

Maybe your stubbornness is keeping you from experiencing something that's actually kind of cool. If you're a nonconformist, then doing what everyone else is doing might go against the very notion of who you take yourself to be. Can you be a nonconformist and still engage people online in a nonconforming way? Maybe, maybe not. But at least ask yourself the question.

I have witnessed powerful friendships and collaborations blossom online. I know people who have collaborated on books together but have never met in person—one pair of authors on SheWrites.com, and another in a Facebook group for mom writers. These are "real" connections, and eventually both of these pairs met in the "real" world and affirmed their admiration and love for each other, which they had already forged through writing and working together and occasional phone check-ins.

At the heart of community is a sense of belonging. You can be in a community, but if you don't belong, you are isolated—either of your own accord or because you've been shunned. News stories abound about how Facebook is used as a tool for bullies. In its anonymity, the Internet does give license to people to act like jerks, no question. I know people who have been stalked and threatened. I have been personally attacked online in the comments sections of my blog posts. There are clear downsides to being active online, so I don't mean to paint a completely rosy picture of Internet culture. But I've also seen love-fests in the form of authors celebrating one another, and hundreds of likes and messages of support during times of struggle and times of great achievement. Online communities do help authors feel less alone in their pursuits, and other people can help you normalize your experiences, if you're brave enough to share what you're going through.

Every summer since 2013, I've held an in-person conference. These have been relatively small affairs, maxing out at around sixty-five participants. The energy in these rooms is palpable, and being with a group for two full days, seeing them, talking with them, engaging with them, is something I look forward to. Yet it's no more powerful for me than my online courses, where people get together on the web or on the phone. Rather than comparing "real" with virtual experiences, I say bring it all on. One is not better than the other. There are myriad ways to connect in the twenty-first century. In past generations, we were limited in the ways we could connect. At first, it was only in person. Later, it was in person or by phone. Today, it's in person or by phone or by Skype or by webinar or by conference line or on social media. That there are all these tendrils of potential connection might be overwhelming, but try not to rank the meaningfulness of various ways you connect with people. All are valuable, and online connections give you a powerful way to leverage how many people you can touch—all through your creative expression, the very thing that drives you as a writer. And that's pretty darn awesome.

Be a Literary Ambassador

One of the things I love about the self-publishing community is how supportive authors are of one another. Yes, plenty of traditionally published authors are supportive and wonderful, too, but indie authors, maybe because they've had to readjust their publishing dreams, maybe because of the ways in which they've had to manifest their own success, tend to rally around one another and other authors in a way that I find inspiring.

The qualities that make you a good literary ambassador are generosity, humility, and the belief that there's enough to go around. At the beginning of this chapter, I mentioned that successful authors find ways to community-build or to create connection. In becoming a literary ambassador, you are doing both. Being a literary ambassador simply means that you are out in the world, actively being inclusive. You do not set yourself apart from the crowd. You become a joiner. This is a foreign concept to people who hate the idea of joining, who see the very idea of seeking out commonalities with others as making themselves anonymous or dull or un-noteworthy. But others see these nonjoiners for what they are: self-important. You can be a successful author and be self-important. There are plenty of examples of these kinds of authors. Some of them even set out to create a divide between themselves and everyone they perceive as lesser than they are. This kind of author is the opposite of a literary ambassador.

One such author is Jonathan Franzen, who was widely criticized for his 2013 *Guardian* article, "What's Wrong with the Modern World?," in which he railed against Amazon and bumbled on about how technology is ruining everything and how the physical book is going on the endangered-species list. (Note: the *Guardian* apparently decided to delete this post from its site, but the archive lives on and can be found easily by Googling its title.) Franzen wrote:

"Amazon wants a world in which books are either self-published or published by Amazon itself, with readers dependent on Amazon reviews in choosing books, and with authors responsible for their own promotion. The work of yakkers and tweeters and braggers, and of people with the money to pay somebody to churn out hundreds of five-star reviews for them, will flourish in that world. But what happens to the people who became writers *because* yakking and tweeting and bragging felt to them like intolerably shallow forms of social engagement? What happens to the people who want to communicate in depth, individual to individual, in the quiet and permanence of the printed word, and who were shaped by their love of writers who wrote when publication still assured some kind of quality control and literary reputations were more than a matter of self-promotional decibel levels?"

What Franzen is doing in this article is embodying a form of specialness. He is setting himself apart from all the shallow masses who are writing not because they love to write or because they yearn to connect through self-expression, but because they're "yakkers" and "braggers" (who are responsible for their own promotion, to boot—the horror of it all!). Franzen deserves to be called out for many things here, and countless authors did take him to task in the aftermath of this truly misguided article, but I want to focus on the degree to which this mindset is anticommunal. It says there is not enough for everyone, and that there are those of us who are worthy and who take this seriously, and then there's everyone else.

For authors like Franzen, scarcity runs in their veins. They're bothered by technology and subscribe to the belief I spoke to at the outset of this chapter that "real" connection happens only one-on-one. "What happens to the people who want to communicate in depth, individual to individual?" But is that what any author is ever doing—communicating individual to individual? The very nature of a book is such that an author communicates to their readers—one, one hundred, one thousand, ten thousand.

Scarcity thinking will kill any hope you have of being or becoming a literary ambassador, because being this person truly means you have to want others to succeed. I have witnessed profound community support among the She Writes Press authors, for instance, who have every right to feel anxious about the fact that their books might compete against one another. But this group of women authors—nearly two hundred strong at the writing of this book—support one another day in and day out in a secret Facebook group and out in the real world, too.

One She Writes Press author told me that if she never makes any money on her book, the reward of publishing it lies in the connections she's made. This group of authors is role-modeling how to be author-ambassadors by cheering one another on, celebrating one another's publication dates, promoting one another online, and showing up to one another's events.

You can still promote the heck out of your own work (and you should), but you must pause to remember that other people's work deserves as much praise and attention as your own (and who better to praise it than you, if you're so moved?), and that another person's success does not lessen the chances of your success. There's enough to go around. There are hundreds and thousands of readers out there who want your book. The ongoing work and challenge is to keep doing what you're doing to find them, reach them, and engage them—over and over again.

Connect with Your Tribe

In 2008, marketer and author Seth Godin wrote a now-famous book called *Tribes: We Need You to Lead Us*. He also did a great TED talk on this topic of tribes that's a worthwhile seventeen-minute use of your time. The premise of the book and the talk has to do with connection. For Godin, a tribe is "any group of people, large or small, who are connected to one another, a leader, and an idea."

The tribe concept is valuable for authors, of course. When an author connects in the right way with their intended audience, they can create true believers and they can create movements—both concepts being key marketing goals and great ways to build an author platform and sell books. When I worked at Seal, the marketing department was always talking about ways to create conversation, and that conversation in itself had the power to become a movement.

As an author, you actually have two tribes. You have the readers you're trying to connect with, who are inspired or moved by or who feel connected to you based on your idea, experience, or story. And you have your fellow authors.

Let's look at your readers first. Whether you're writing fiction or memoir or self-help, you want to try to identify an issue or a topic at the heart of your book that readers will connect with. Prescriptive-nonfiction authors usually have an easy time with this exercise because their books are typically idea- or issue-driven. Memoirists and novelists, on the other hand, don't always understand how an idea or an issue rallies readers. But pinpoint one of your favorite books and ask yourself what it was you loved about it. I loved *The Handmaid's Tale* for its distinctly feminist point of view and message; I loved *Drinking: A Love Story* for its nuanced exploration of the author's relationship with alcohol; I loved *Sarah's Key* for its depiction of the Holocaust's ripple effect and post-traumatic impact on a survivor. The tribes these authors created, at their most basic, would be feminists; drinkers interested in examining their relationship to alcohol; and readers interested in Nazi Germany. It's possible that there are other tribes connected to these books, but this is what drew me to each of them and made me a true believer, so much so that I now recommend these books often to others.

Do not underestimate the tribe that is your fellow authors. I mentioned the powerful community of She Writes Press authors—this is a quantifiable group of women all connected by the fact that they're published on the same imprint. Other writing communities worth taking a look at are genre writers. They know who they are, and they support one another. They know they're part of the same tribe, and they honor that connection. If you start observing romance writers or sci-fi writers or YA authors, you'll start to notice the social connections—through social media, speaking circuits, blogging on each other's sites, and more.

Thinking about the people you want to connect with is an incredibly valuable exercise, but it's important to note that the way in which you think about connecting to your readers is inevitably ego-based. And it should be! You need to reach deep inside and touch that part of you that wants to be huge. Some of you will have no problem with this kind of visualization, while others will be mortified by the very thought of it. But if you want to connect with a tribe, you want to have true believers. That means being a leader and creating a conversation that others want to be a part of. At this point, you become a leader because you are the initiator of this conversation. Or you are the holder of the original idea that prompted the conversation, and so you have fans. And what author doesn't want this? So it's okay to have a little ego in the game.

Where your connection to other authors is concerned, however, you basically need to strip away ego. You need to make these interactions all about others. There has to be space for more than one idea and more than one leader. Truly supporting the vision of another means being giving and rallying behind their idea. If anyone doubts that there can be more than one leader in the same space, or thinks that supporting the idea of another comes at the expense of your own idea, it's important to try to uncover the root of this belief system. There are countless examples in big business of rival companies, and we all know that competition is good for consumers. The same is true in book publishing—there's room for all the authors you love, right? And when you become an author yourself, these people whom you've always admired become your peers.

While you still might go gaga over the literary greats you've always loved, it can feel a little more difficult to support newbie authors coming up alongside you or following in your wake. However, don't lose sight of the extent to which these writers—especially if they're writing about the same idea, experience, or story—are your people. Befriend them. If you were to forge a strong connection, who knows where the relationship might lead—to future joint appearances or collaborations; to referring each other if one of you isn't available for a speaking gig; to recommending each other's books to your audiences. I've seen every one of these things happen as a result of heartfelt support.

One of the best examples I've witnessed of writers connecting happened between Amy Ferris and Hollye Dexter, who met online and forged a friendship, communicating by e-mail and eventually by phone. Ferris was already a published memoirist (*Marrying George Clooney*). Her second book was an anthology that she coedited with Dexter, and that was only the first of many collaborations. The two have toured together and worked together on subsequent projects. Ferris championed Dexter to publish her own memoir, *Fire Season*, and Dexter contributed an essay to Ferris's subsequent book, a single-editor anthology. And I have no doubt that their joint ventures will continue.

When I saw Elizabeth Gilbert speak at the 2014 Wake Up Festival in Colorado, she told a story of walking up to Ann Patchett and telling her straight-up, "I love you!" Here was Gilbert, an internationally best-selling author, going completely knock-kneed over a fellow writer. Gilbert was writing her own novel at the time, and she could have seen Patchett as a rival, but instead the two went on to forge a beautiful friendship through letter writing.

Tribes are founded on shared ideas and values, so if you find someone out there who's writing about your ideas and who embodies your values, embrace them. If you are in connection with someone who threatens you because their work is overlapping with yours or because they always seem to show up in the space you're trying to dominate, support them. If they drive you crazy, you don't have to befriend them, but it can only benefit you to be in connection with those writers who share your ideas and values. When you operate from a mindset that there is always enough to go around, you will discover that being connected with other writers in your space will actually grow your readership, your own platform, and your visibility. After all, people are not looking to connect with a single person, or for a single leader whose ideas are gospel. We all crave and want multiple points of view, and to connect with ideas that inspire us. The first step in starting your movement is to get abundantly clear about your idea or topic, and about whom you want to reach or connect with, and then to remain open. The only control you have over the outcome of your particular effort to create a movement is in doing what you do the best you can, and in staying responsive, engaging, and supportive of others.

Chapter 10.

Green Light, Go

I wrote in the introduction of this book that while readers have stopped looking to the big houses to be the curators of the lists they want to read, aspiring authors have not made this same leap. It may be a revelation that all readers really care about is a good book. They're not paying attention to which house published the work; they're paying attention to the quality—the story or subject matter, the editorial execution, the cover and interior design, the print quality.

And while the dream of being picked up by a big house is certainly one of the things that you need to dismantle before you can effectively green-light your book, there are others as well. You may have a fantasy that your book will be met with a rush of affection and that editors will swarm to place their highest bids as your manuscript gets rushed off to auction. You may have concerns about money: you don't have it; you can't or don't want to spend the amount required to give your book a fighting chance. There's the validation part: you really need other people to tell you that your efforts are worthwhile, that you're not making a mistake, that you're not going to regret your decision later. There's fear of failure and fear of success: What if the book fails miserably? What if you embarrass yourself? What if the book does well? What if the anonymity and smallness you've been unwittingly cultivating end up pushing you into something you don't feel ready for? There are commitment issues: You're in and then you're out. You're riding the fence, sometimes for years. The clock is ticking, but you can't make a decision. There's all this and more.

Try not to judge yourself for those things that are standing in your way, but do assess what they are so you can take a step forward. You can ride the fence for a while, but at some point a reality starts to kick in: the time you've spent sitting and deliberating your publishing options could have been better spent writing new material! I know people who've spent a decade, literally, trying to figure out how to publish. They have a finished book, and it's still sitting there. This is the definition of inertia, folks. Ten years can pass in the blink of an eye, and you'll soon find yourself a decade older, without having done the thing you said you wanted to do. If you saved $5 a week for ten years, you'd have $2,600, enough to finance a print book.

When I give writers guidance about the world of traditional publishing, I tell them not to wait more than six months for an agent's or editor's response. If an agent sits on your work for six months, they don't want it; they're not enthusiastic enough to represent you well. I extend the same advice in your approach to yourself and whether you're enthusiastic enough about your own work to give it the green light. If you're debating what to do for longer than six months, you need to make a decision. You need to either publish or set your project aside and start something fresh, something you will care enough about to green-light. If you start something new and the old project keeps tugging at your heartstrings, then you know. It wants to see the light of day, and you have a duty to yourself as a writer to allow it to breathe, to be read, to be published—even if you serialize it on your blog, even if you publish it only as an e-book.

Consider your own internal stoplight for a moment. Is the light red? Or yellow? If it's green, are you sitting at the light, hesitating to step on the gas? Do yourself the favor of unpacking what's here for you and getting emotionally sorted out before you say yes. Because once you do say yes, you want to be all the way in. You want your foot on the gas, full tank, ready to go, without reservations.

Once You're Ready . . .

When you've made the decision to do it, what lies ahead of you are a number of paths, and you must choose which one you want to take. As we discussed in Chapter 1, there are multiple ways to publish, and you choose the method and your team.

You might decide that hybrid publishing is an interesting option. Talk to the publishers at these houses. Connect with authors who've published with them. You might decide on agent-assisted self-publishing. Same thing. Ask if you can speak to other authors about their experiences. Buy books the press you're considering has published. Feel the quality of the books. Read a couple and make sure you feel comfortable joining their ranks.

If you decide to self-publish, hire someone to help you think through the big picture, or get a mentor. You want to work with someone who will be honest with you about your cover and interior design and the editorial readiness of your manuscript. Don't be a renegade and do this fully on your own, with no input from someone who's been to the rodeo before. There's too much at stake, and you can avoid amateur mistakes at very little cost to you by hiring someone for an hour to eyeball what you have and give you feedback.

Decide up front whether you have money to spend on publicity. If you do, start interviewing publicists six months to a full year before your book comes out. Give yourself and them plenty of lead time. Come up with a plan and a timeline. Consider how many advance reader copies you'll send out, and whether you'll submit to review outlets like *Publishers Weekly*, *Kirkus*, and *Booklist*. Make sure you know what your expectations are, and clarify them to your publicist. It's too late post-publication to decide that your publicity expectations were actually higher than you made them out to be.

Once you decide to green-light your work, let people know you're going to publish. Share the news. Announce it online. Brag a little. If you're working with a company that's doing the services for you, get a sense of how soon the cover process might start. If you're self-publishing, start the cover process as soon as possible. Nothing makes publishing more tangible than having a cover. I have three print books (including this one) and an e-book, and in all four cases I had my cover design completed early in the process. It's served as a motivation and has reminded me that the book I'm working on really is going to end up being a book. Getting started on your cover design concretizes your goal and helps keep you grounded and focused on the finish line.

Once you've gathered your team—which may include an editor, a designer, a publicist, and a strategist or consultant—or, if you're working with a publisher, their team, make sure you understand what's expected of you and where you should be focusing your time leading up to publication. If you're not finished with your book, that obviously needs to come first. But after it's done, your publicist or a marketing expert can help you attend to your social media platforms, grow your platform, and get more of your content published (both online and print). Your publicist will send out advance reader copies of your book in order to try to garner reviews. If you're self-publishing, you'll have to remember to upload your reviews to Amazon yourself as they come in; if you're working with a publisher, don't assume they're seeing every review. Work with them to make sure your Amazon page stays up to date.

As you approach publication, and after your book comes out, you may have other kinds of media hits and opportunities, including book tours, radio and television spots, interviews, and excerpts syndicated online and in print. Nothing about indie publishing is limiting or less than traditional publishing. The authors we publish at She Writes Press, and other authors I know who've indie-published, have secured trade reviews, been on TV, had their work reviewed in major glossy magazines, and been featured in national newspapers. Green-lighting your work is a mindset, and from there what flows is fully up to you and depends on how big you want to go. Sales are not necessarily commensurate with the time and resources you put behind your book, but if you're in it for the journey and for what's possible, and if you say yes to any opportunity that brings you more visibility, you are pulling your weight, and there's no telling where your journey will lead you.

The New Gatekeepers

Because publishers can no longer be relied upon to shape the cultural conversation based on their literary choices, readers have become the new gatekeepers. Readers are smart and voracious, and they find all kinds of ways to share the books they love with their friends and larger communities. It used to be said that word of mouth could make a book; now word of mouth is amplified by social media and platforms dedicated exclusively to promoting books. Amazon is a search engine that uses keywords to help you find books on topics you care about. Goodreads allows you to browse reviews by your friends. BookBub and other sites dedicated to promoting e-books give you access to thousands of readers in exchange for lowering your book's price to 99 cents for a limited period of time.

We talked about discoverability in Chapter 8, and here I'm reminding you how encouraging it is that so many people out there are committed to helping other people find books they want to read. As an author, you can't say yes to everything, but you must say yes to some things. You want to pick and choose the promotional opportunities that make sense to you, or the platforms and creative angles that excite you. Many She Writes Press authors have done BookBub campaigns, and the number of downloads they've gotten has been energizing and rewarding to them. Others have hired private marketing people to help them get better rankings on Amazon. Some have focused their attention on social media strategy, creating memes to spread the word about their message and their books. A couple have even attempted to home in on celebrities, believing that if the right person were to be captured holding their book in a photo, or if they could get an endorsement or a tweet from a big name, that would be the game-changer they're looking for.

This hasn't happened to a She Writes Press author yet, but it happened on my watch at Seal Press, when our sister imprint, Running Press, published *Skinny Bitch*, which went on to become a *New York Times* best seller after Victoria Beckham was photographed holding the book, title face out, in her beach attire while on summer vacation. The book went gangbusters, and history was made. I wouldn't recommend putting a lot of time or energy into this strategy, unless you know someone who can make something like this happen without its seeming completely inauthentic—like a B-list celebrity holding up your book while posing and staring straight at the camera. The genius of the Beckham shot, which was pure luck for those authors, was that she was actually reading this book, so the endorsement lay in the capture of an insider moment, the equivalent of seeing what was on her nightstand.

The best way to influence the success of your own book directly is to get Amazon reviews. This is no easy task, but fifty reviews is a goal you can set for yourself. Fifty Amazon reviews will bump you up into a new bracket of visibility on Amazon, based on the algorithms they have set up, which make Amazon the powerful recommendation engine it is. Don't stop submitting your work to reviews and contests, either—the ones you qualify to submit to, at least. Your book's success hinges on how often it pops up. When I see a book reviewed once, I'm likely to move on and not take much notice. But if I see that same title reviewed again and again across multiple review sites—even small ones—I'm going to recognize the title and the cover and start to pay attention. Industry professionals work in the same way. Editors, librarians, book buyers, and reps all zero in on the same thing: repeated exposure. Your publicist is largely responsible for getting your book out to review outlets, but you can supplement their efforts by doing your own research and mailings and follow-up, especially if you're on a limited budget or once your campaign has come to a close.

That the book industry is the new Wild West is good for tireless authors, those who thrive on puzzles and research and list building. If this is not your thing, hire out. Don't burden yourself with things you aren't good at. Consider what you do well, exploit that, and let your team carry the rest.

The fact that the industry's state of massive flux has brought about this shift of power is a great thing for indie authors. When readers are gatekeepers, all of us have a shot at success. Readers come to your work without bias, so the onus is on you to wow them—to write the best book you can write, and then to let it be received as it will be received. Alice Walker said something similar, only far more eloquently: "Make your writing an offering to the world. Let the world do with it as it will."

Have a Plan, Leverage What You Have, and Keep Writing

Earlier in this chapter, I urged you to consider whether you have a budget for publicity. In fact, you need to consider your overall budget and what you're willing to invest in your book project. I've known authors who've wished, after the fact, that they had invested more. I've known authors who've been pissed off about having to spend any money and who should have worked out their emotions about that before they entered into a publishing agreement. Knowing the costs and coming to terms with them are important. Having a budget will also help you determine which indie publishing path you should be on—which is mandated somewhat by what kind of money you can allocate.

When you indie-publish, you set the tone, both with your expectations and with your financial investment. This is not to say you can buy success. Yes, I've heard of authors cheating the system and buying up their own copies on Amazon and through bookstores in order to land on the *New York Times* best-seller list, but these authors end up with hundreds of books in their garage that they have to either sell or give away. There is nothing feel-good about this. Authors who need to buy their way onto a best-seller list are definitely not adhering to the code of ethics outlined in the preceding chapter, and they likely wouldn't bother to read this book anyway.

Being a realist about how many books you will probably sell is a hard pill to swallow. In 2013, Nick Morgan reported for Forbes.com that self-published books, on average, sell fewer than 250 copies; other outlets reported even fewer than that. In 2015, Lynn Neary reported a story on NPR called "When It Comes to Book Sales, What Counts as Success Might Surprise You," whose message boiled down to the fact that traditional publishing's sales aren't nearly as good as most people believe them to be. Literary agent Jane Dystel, interviewed for the piece, said, "A sensational sale would be about 25,000 copies. Even

15,000 would be a strong enough sale to get the author's attention for a second book." Notice she said the word "sensational," not "common."

Author Barry Eisler, a self-publishing advocate, was also interviewed and made the important point that while it's true that "most self-published authors aren't able to make a living from their writing, it's also absolutely true of legacy publishing. It's always been that way."

In traditional publishing, failing means not earning out your advance. In self-publishing, failing could be taken to mean not earning back your expenses. But the question then needs to be: Over what period of time? In traditional publishing, you have a one-year window, and sometimes, in bigger houses, even less. But in self-publishing, you can take your sweet time in terms of thinking about the long-term payoff of your book—and you should, because the real financial gains will come after a second or even a third book.

Most aspiring and first-time authors, in my experience, have unrealistic expectations about sales. The vast majority think it will be easy to sell through at least one thousand copies of their book. After all, one thousand seems like a really small number when you look at best-seller lists and see books that are selling over one thousand copies per day. Actually, it's not easy to sell this many copies. As a result, you might adopt a strategy in which you temper your expectations for a first book and then increase your efforts (and financial investment) with each subsequent book you write, as you build up your inventory and your backlist.

In my work with authors, I encourage them to play big while also entering into their publishing endeavor with their eyes wide open. Part of the reason I urge authors to think bigger is that I find that too many authors are (still) holding themselves back from their own success. They are waiting for someone to give them the green light, when in fact they are the only ones who can do that. Authors who are suffering because someone told them no are really only saying no to themselves. And this is not just about getting published; it's about the bigger picture of what happens after your book comes out. You can say yes to yourself by self-publishing but still say no to marketing, no to putting yourself out there, no to being as successful as you want to be.

In 2014, I had one of the She Writes Press authors over to my office to sign her contract in person. I asked her about her marketing plan, and she said she didn't have one. I prodded, wanting to know why. She said that she'd been working on her book for five years and was ready just to get it out there. She didn't care whether it was successful or not. When I inquired into this more deeply, she paused. It took a few moments, but she confessed that maybe she'd been talking herself into believing that her book couldn't be successful. She'd used a lot of brainpower, it turned out, telling herself that it would be okay if the book did not succeed and that it was enough just to publish it.

I'm happy to report that this author has changed her tune. She hired a publicist in the end, and her book got good media attention and has seen better-than-average sales. I appreciated her ability to admit what was going on for her, though, and saying it out loud was what led to her being able to reassess her mindset about her book's potential for success.

As you embark upon your publishing journey, you'll hear a lot about "playing big," and there's a lot of pressure to do so. But playing big is not about impressing others or necessarily about making money or getting famous (though in book publishing, these things can be the result of playing big). It's about honoring yourself to live into your full potential. Playing big is the opposite of keeping yourself small because you're afraid of failure.

Poet David Whyte has a wonderful quote that I've had in the signature line of my e-mail for years now. It says, "Anything or anyone that does not bring you alive is too small for you." Sometimes we need a reality check. Sometimes, if we can't see how we're limiting ourselves, we need someone else to pry us out of our limited perspective so that we can see something bigger, broader, more expansive. Green-lighting your work is one of the most exciting decisions you'll ever make, but we each need to decide for ourselves whether and when we're going to leap. And once you do, look forward, not back. Give yourself the gifts of legitimacy, validation, and authority. If you've come this far, you've earned it.

Acknowledgments

This book was written in response to the many good questions posed to me by She Writes Press authors. I could not have written it without SheWrites.com and She Writes Press— the authors and my team, especially Crystal Patriarche, Kamy Wicoff, Caitlyn Levin, Lauren Wise, Krissa Lagos, and Julie Metz. Thank you to Annie Tucker, the most amazing coach and editor, who was with me chapter by chapter, for her astute comments and constant championing. And Tabitha Lahr, for her beautiful design work and unwavering patience. I'm lucky to be part of an amazing writing community, and I am thankful to all the many authors and experts who let me use their stories and who inspire me with their tenacity and generosity. I am thankful for the perspective I've gained about publishing, and while I share some hard critiques of traditional publishing in these pages, I'm thankful to so many people in this industry. I have been supported, mentored, and encouraged at each step of my career, and I've been beyond grateful for the industry's positive response to She Writes Press and our nontraditional model. That there are so many book people and industry insiders who truly get what we're doing is wind in my sails, and I appreciate that there are so many people who are looking with hope and excitement to this publishing middle ground that She Writes Press and many other hybrid publishers occupy. I want to thank Ingram Publisher Services for believing in She Writes Press, and the countless indie bookstores nationwide that embrace our model and love our authors enough to regularly order our books and have us back for events over and over again. Thanks to all of you for your support. Finally, I'm grateful to my family, especially my wife, Krista, my cheerleader, proofreader, thought-stoker, and coparent, without whom I would not find the time or space to write a single word.

About the Author

photo by Reenie Raschke

Brooke Warner is publisher of She Writes Press, president of Warner Coaching Inc., author of *What's Your Book?*, *Green-Light Your Book*, and *How to Sell Your Memoir*, and co-author of *Breaking Ground on Your Memoir*. Brooke's expertise is in traditional and new publishing. She is the former executive editor of Seal Press and sits on the boards of the Independent

Book Publishers Association, the Bay Area Book Festival, and the National Association of Memoir Writers. She blogs actively on *Huffington Post* Books and SheWrites.com. She lives and works in Berkeley, California.

Websites:

www.brookewarner.com

www.shewritespress.com

www.writeyourmemoirinsixmonths.com

Social media:

 warnercoaching

 brooke_warner

 linkedin.com/in/warnercoaching

 warnercoaching

SELECTED TITLES FROM SHE WRITES PRESS

She Writes Press is an independent publishing
company founded to serve women writers everywhere.
Visit us at www.shewritespress.com.

What's Your Book? A Step-by-Step Guide to Get You from Inspiration to Published Author by Brooke Warner. $12.95, 978-1-938314-00-1. An aspiring author's go-to guide for getting from idea to publication.

Journey of Memoir: The Three Stages of Memoir Writing by Linda Joy Myers. $22.95, 978-1-938314-26-1. A straightforward, highly effective workbook designed to help memoirists of every level get their story on the page.

Breaking Ground on Your Memoir by Linda Joy Myers and Brooke Warner. $14.95, 978-1-631520-85-3. Myers and Warner present from the ground up—from basic to advanced—the craft and skills memoirists can draw upon to write a powerful and moving story, as well as inspiration to write, finish, and polish their own story.

Three Minus One: Parents' Stories of Love & Loss edited by Sean Hanish and Brooke Warner. $17.95, 978-1-938314-80-3. A collection of stories and artwork by parents who have suffered child loss that offers insight into this unique and devastating experience.

The Thriver's Edge: Seven Keys to Transform the Way You Live, Love, and Lead by Donna Stoneham. $16.95, 978-1-63152-980-1. A "coach in a book" from master executive coach and leadership expert Dr. Donna Stoneham, *The Thriver's Edge* outlines a practical road map to breaking free of the barriers keeping you from being everything you're capable of being.

Where Have I Been All My Life? A Journey Toward Love and Wholeness by Cheryl Rice. $16.95, 978-1-63152-917-7. Rice's universally relatable story of how her mother's sudden death launched her on a journey into the deepest parts of grief—and, ultimately, toward love and wholeness.